CW00518741

PLAIN TRUTHS
ABOUT LIFE, FAITH
AND HEALING

About the Author

The Revd Canon Roy Lawrence

After National Service in the Army, Roy read Classics and Theology at Oxford and Cambridge. He was ordained in 1959 and served his curacy at St George's Stockport. He went on to be Vicar of All Saints, Thelwall (1962-68); then St George's Hyde (1968-75); and finally St Stephen's and St Alban's in Prenton, Birkenhead (1975-1996) – all in the Chester Diocese. He was made an Honorary Canon in 1986.

For the first six years of retirement, Roy was Co-ordinator for all the Advisors in the Christian Healing Ministry for all the denominations of the churches in the UK (in association with the Acorn Foundation).

Throughout his ministry, Roy and his wife, Eira, travelled to many places leading conferences, missions and 'days away', both in the UK and overseas.

A popular Christian writer and broadcaster, Roy has written 14 books on the subject of divine healing and prayer. He was active as a trustee to Christian charities The Plain Truth and Flame Christian & Community Radio (CCR) right up until he died on 25 April 2018 aged 86.

PLAIN TRUTHS
ABOUT LIFE, FAITH
AND HEALING

A collection of inspirational articles

Roy Lawrence

www.plain-truth.org.uk

The Plain Truth (Cambridge)

The Plain Truth

© 2019 The Plain Truth. All rights reserved.

No part of this book may be reproduced in any form without written permission from The Plain Truth Ltd, 15 Meadowlands, Burwell, Cambridge CB25 0HG.

The Plain Truth (Ltd) is a registered charity (No. 1098217) and a Company limited by guarantee (No. 4619778).

The Plain Truth is a registered trademark in the UK. Published by: The Plain Truth, 15 Meadowlands, Burwell, Cambridge CB25 0HG.

Email: *mail@plaintruth.co.uk*
Web: *www.plain-truth.org.uk*

Cover design: The Plain Truth

Cover photo: Christopher Lawrence

First edition 2019
ISBN: 978-1-912804-95-5

A catalogue record for this book is available from the British Library.

Printed and bound in the UK, April 2019, by Biddles Books Ltd, King's Lynn, Norfolk.

Contents

Foreword

I am delighted and very privileged to have been asked to write the Foreword to this collection of Roy Lawrence's articles which were previously published in The Plain Truth[1] magazine.

For I have known, loved, and admired Roy for more than thirty years. I first met him and his wife Eira through an organisation called the Acorn Christian Healing Trust, of which Roy was a leading light and later became an Honorary Consultant, together with Anne Long, who inspired the ministry of Christian Listening, which has proved to be a powerful source of healing for many.

Roy has been a long-time champion of the ministry of Christian Healing, through listening, prayer, the laying on of hands, and worship. He has always been sensitive to the pain of life and sought to be a channel of God's grace and comfort, both to individuals and through his relevant, down-to-earth articles for The Plain Truth, as well as his broadcasts for stations such as Flame CCR.[2]

Some of you who read this book may not know that Roy has written a number of short, readable books on healing and the Christian life which you can find on the internet.

Roy and Eira spent a number of holidays with my wife Judy and me in our home on the Isle of Man and he taught me so much. We spoke too during his Dark Night of the Soul experience and he kindly sent me a draft of his article which would later appear in The Plain Truth – I still have that draft. (You can read this article on page 67.) I believe that only very special people (those who can cope with it and understand it) are given a glimpse of what Jesus felt in the Garden of Gethsemane or perhaps when He cried out: 'My God, my God, why have you forsaken me?'

Roy was always sensitive to the pain of people, which he could see in the faces at church, on the bus, in the street. People damaged by upbringing, bad relationships, being let down and so on. He sought to reach out to them with the healing power of Christ through articles in The Plain Truth and in many other ways.

Although sadly Roy is no longer with us, I pray that this collection of his writings will be a source of healing, comfort and hope in the days to come.

Jim Noakes

About Jim Noakes: Jim set up and was CEO of the Financial Supervision Commission in the Isle of Man until he retired in 1998. He was also active in the Church, being a Licensed Reader in the Church of England at St Ninian's, Douglas. He and his wife were in charge of a church planted by St Ninian's in a pub (*The Cat With No Tail*) in Douglas for more than 20 years. In 2012 he received Maundy Money from Her Majesty the Queen as the representative of the Diocese of Sodor & Man in her Diamond Jubilee year.

ENDNOTES

1 The Plain Truth (*www.plain-truth.org.uk*) is a Christian charity which produces a free magazine that is sent to almost 80 countries worldwide. Up until his death, as well as a long-time author, Roy Lawrence was also a trustee of the charity.

2 Flame Christian and Community Radio (Flame CCR, *www.flameradio.org*) is a community radio station broadcasting since 2009 full-time on medium wave in Merseyside and world-wide on the internet. As well as being a broadcaster on Flame CCR, Roy Lawrence was also a trustee of its operating charity Wirral Christian Media.

Preface[1]

All of the material in this book originally appeared in The Plain Truth – an English Christian magazine – which has been reborn in recent years. It now occupies a central place in the life of the Churches in Britain and beyond. Its contents are wide-ranging and sometimes very significant.

I count it a privilege to be numbered amongst its regular contributors. The editor, John Halford[2] now lives in the USA, and the managing editor, Mary Hammond,[3] lives in England. If they will have it, I dedicate this book to them and do so with gratitude for the work they do for our Lord, for His Church and for the Kingdom of God.

Roy Lawrence

ENDNOTES

1 Roy Lawrence wrote this Preface and the outline chapters of this book he intended to publish prior to 2008. It was discovered after his death in 2018, and permission to publish was granted by his widow, Eira.
2 John Halford remained as Editor until 2008 when he took the role of Consulting Editor up until his death on 21 October 2014.
3 Mary Hammond took over the role of Editor from John Halford in September 2008.

PART ONE:
PLAIN TRUTHS ABOUT LIFE

Enjoy being unique!

If you and I had been created on the mass-production line of some factory or other, then we would probably be much the same as each other. But we are not. After God made you and me, he then broke the mould. There is no one in the whole world exactly like you or me. There never has been – there never will be. We are unique – and we are meant to enjoy it.

This is true at every level of our being. For instance, your body is not identical to anybody else's. Nobody has exactly the same fingerprints that you have. Nobody has precisely the same DNA.

You are also unique in mind. Human minds differ in innumerable ways. Some are artistic. Some are scientific. Some are introverts. Some are extraverts. Some are good with their heads. Others are good with their hands. We all have different aptitudes, capabilities and interests. Never put yourself down because you can't do what others can. You will be able to do what they can't.

Above all, we are unique in spirit. This must be so because the Bible tells us that men and women were created 'in the image of God'[1] and the one thing we know above all about God is that he is certainly unique.

So you and I have been given a life, an identity, a destiny which is like no other. Never ever despise yourself. For that would be to despise the God in whose image you have been wonderfully made and whose nature you mysteriously share.

Of course, the Bible also tells us that the image of God has become flawed and distorted in us. We are sinners and we need to be saved from our sins and from the terrible consequences which those sins can so easily have, both in time and in eternity. But the good news of the Christian faith is that though our sins can destroy us they do not need to do so. God has not ceased to love us. Though we are sinners, we are precious sinners, and if we have put our trust in Jesus as our Saviour, we can know God's forgiveness and re-creative power, and we can and should marvel at all that, by the grace of God, we are called to be and to do and to become.

We should marvel too at each new day that God gives us. For it has the potential to be just as unique as we are.

Each new day

Ronald Brown, formerly Bishop of Birkenhead, used to recommend to his clergy an old and little-known devotional work called *Hogg's Morning Meditation*. Here are some words from it which I sometimes incorporate into my own morning prayers:

'Say to thy soul: "Soul, wait awhile! Enter not so heedlessly upon thy daily round.

Bethink thee, this is a day which it hath cost God long ages to fashion forth. For it had to grow out of yesterday – out of thy doings, and others' doings, and his own thought and help and patience, throughout the hours that now are yesterday and all the days that went to make of yesterday what yesterday was. Wherefore this day, which seemeth to thee so like unto other days that thy acquired capabilities and experience might suffice for competent discharge of its affairs, is indeed not like but different. It is God's newest handiwork, the fruit of his longest patience. Darest thou lay on it thy clumsy fingers, until first, in the quiet, his commission shall have sounded in thine ears afresh?"'

In much the same vein Thomas Carlyle wrote, 'Here hath been dawning another blue day. Think – wilt thou let it slip useless away?' The Roman poet Horace advised his readers, *carpe diem* – 'snatch the day', maximize it, use it to the full, enjoy its uniqueness.

What you do matters

Also if each new day is unique, so is every new assignment which life brings us, whether great or small. One of the most important lessons which I have ever learned in my life was taught me quite casually when I was serving as a curate and part-time hospital chaplain. One day I was visiting one of the wards for which I was responsible in the old Stockport Infirmary, when I came across a local football referee, who happened to be a patient there. He had a high reputation as a referee and I told him so. I have never forgotten his reply. He said, 'I do have a secret and it's this. Every time I referee a match, I do so as if it were the only match I will ever referee in my whole life.'

It was like a flash of lightning. Suddenly I saw how this must apply to my own ministry.

I must do just the same thing. Every wedding, every funeral, every baptism, every Sunday service which came my way must be unique. I must take each one as though it were the only one I would ever take in my life.

This is a principle which has served me well – and I apply the same principle to every article I write for The Plain Truth.

You can work out for yourself how it applies to you. Whether you are starting a day's work or sitting down to write a letter, or going into the kitchen to bake a cake, or doing any of the million and one things that are part and parcel of life – you can make it unique, because it is.

You can do your day's work or write the letter, or bake the cake, or do whatever it may be, as though it is the only time you will ever do it.

And if all these apparently humdrum things can properly be regarded as unique, how much more so is this true of each relationship.

Special relationships

Every relationship which we have – ranging from the close relationship of husband and wife, or parent and child, or intimate friends with each other to the more casual contacts we continually have with neighbours and colleagues and folk we happen to bump into at work or socially – is unique.

It must be so, because if you are unique and I am unique then any relationship we may have together must be doubly so. Every relationship has the capacity to be special – and of course this includes the relationship which we have with Jesus, if we have invited him into our lives. This, I think, may be the meaning of the mysterious text in the Book of Revelation, in which Jesus promises, 'I will give each one a white stone on which is written a new name, which no one knows except the one who receives it.'[2]

If I am right, the white stone and the new name represent the highly personal and individual nature of the relationship which we are each called to have with our Lord.

Our salvation, like our souls, is individually fashioned, not mass-produced. It is as unique as we are. You are special and so is your relationship with Jesus.

Value yourself

So next time somebody tries to put you down – as people will from time to time – inside yourself you can give a chuckle and say: 'Sorry, mate. Sorry you are the sort of sad person who needs to put others down, but in my case I take my self-regard not from the likes of you but from the God who made me (and he does not make rubbish), who loves me (so much that he gave his Son Jesus to be my Saviour) and who calls me to do and to be and to become something quite unique for him.'

Here is one final Biblical text to hammer the point home. Ephesians 2:10 says that we are God's 'workmanship' and the Greek word for 'workmanship' is *poiema* – God's poem.

Wouldn't it be wonderful if Shakespeare were to rise from the dead and write your biography?

Well, the good news is that you have a greater

biographer than Shakespeare – none other than God himself. You are God's poetic creation. So enjoy being unique. Value all that God has put into you, each new day, each project, each relationship.

And remember, because eternity lies ahead, we don't know the half of it yet!

📖 PUBLISHED IN THE PLAIN TRUTH: APRIL – MAY 2007

ENDNOTES

1 Genesis 1:2 6-27
2 Revelation 2:17

Don't forget to say 'Thank You'

B ack in the days when I was a student at Oxford, my life was influenced to a considerable degree by one of the local clergy. He was a small man but his ministry was by no means small. His name was Canon Keith de Berry and he was the Rector of St Aldate's Church. Hundreds of my contemporaries were touched by him. We still thank God for him today. I remember going to him once and asking him what advice he would give to anyone who wanted to have a happy life. His answer came instantly – 'Cultivate a spirit of thankfulness'.

He was absolutely right in this as in so much else. Nobody can find happiness by pursuing it directly. Happiness is a by-product. It comes almost incidentally from a range of other factors, of which one of the most important is a spirit of thankfulness.

In past issues of The Plain Truth we have looked at some of the main ingredients of effective prayer. Traditionally, there are four of these and they are easy to remember because their first letters spell out the word ACTS –

Adoration, Confession, Thanksgiving and Supplication. Adoration means acknowledging and marvelling at the nature of God. Confession means coming clean about our own nature. Supplication means asking for things both for ourselves and for others. In previous issues we have already thought about these three types of prayer.

So far, however, we have not thought together about 'thanksgiving' and it is now time to put that right, because we really do diminish ourselves and our prayers if we leave it out.

The 'little and large' approach

Adequate prayers of thanksgiving require a bit of thought in advance. Otherwise we may find that we are so preoccupied with our own needs and worries and fancies that the prayers which say 'thank you' just get crowded out by other things. One suggestion which you may find helpful is to try a 'little and large' approach to thanking God for your blessings. Start by identifying some of the little things in life which give you pleasure and do you good. They might include the smile which the postman gives you, the flowers in your local park, the way your wheelie-bin is emptied regularly by council employees, the enjoyment your favourite TV programme gives you, and much more besides. Let your mind range around the small-sized blessings of life. You may be surprised how many of them there are.

Then move on to some of the larger things in life for which you have even greater cause to be thankful. They could include the gift of life itself, the amazing universe in which we find ourselves, planet Earth which is God's special gift to humankind, the wonder of nature, the love of those who are near and dear to us, and the love which God himself has shown to us by the gift of his Son Jesus and of the Gospel which Christ lived and died to bring to us. You may find it meaningful to consolidate your act of thanksgiving by using the words of one of the hymns of gratitude, either a traditional one like the old German hymn *Nun danket alle Gott*, which we sing in its English version Now thank we all our God, or a more modern worship-song such as Alison Huntley's *Thank you Jesus, thank you Jesus, thank you Lord for loving me*.

Alphabet of thanksgiving

If you are prepared to spend a little more time expressing your gratitude to God, one way of doing so is to construct a whole alphabet of thanksgiving. This involves going through the letters of the alphabet and working out something or someone for whom each letter can stand.

For example, if I were to construct a personal alphabet of thanksgiving here and now (and it is something which I do from time to time in my own prayer-life), 'A' might remind me of Albert, my former churchwarden and loyal friend. He worked faithfully with me for years when I was vicar of St George's Hyde, and because he was the local photographer, I still treasure dozens of photographs which he took of local events.

'B' could stand for the Bible in my alphabet of thanksgiving. We should be so grateful that we have a God who communicates with us and for the Bible as one of his primary channels of communication. I might also find myself thinking of other books which have been precious to me over the years. Moreover, as an author myself, I do thank God for the publishers who have accepted the risk of taking on my own books.

The letter 'C' often brings me to thank God for my older son, Christopher. I find myself thanking God that he has made a success of his profession, that he has a devoted wife and three talented children, and that he is a better father than I ever was myself! And just in case my younger son, Paul, should read this article, I can assure him that he comes up equally regularly under the letter 'P'. Both our children are loving to their mother and to me and we are truly grateful for their love.

'D' could remind me that the curates who have worked with me in parish ministry have included four Davids, a Donald and a lovely woman priest called Debbie, who died at a tragically early age, but not before she had offered a truly remarkable ministry both to our parish and to me.

'E' must stand for my wife Eira. I could not have wished for a better marriage partner. After Jesus himself, Eira is certainly the most important person in my life and God's greatest gift to me. I can never be sufficiently grateful to him for her.

'F' could stand for so many good things – the food I eat, the family and friends who mean so much to me, the Faith which stands at the heart of my life and work, and much more besides. Take your pick.

As for 'G', there is God himself! I remember a child's prayer which I came across years ago. 'Look after yourself, God, because, if anything happens to you, we're sunk!' And so the alphabet of thanksgiving goes on. Of course yours will be completely different, but you will be surprised how easily the letters will come to life for you. You need not even be intimidated by the letter 'X'. I have found several things which X can stand for, and not least the X which I put on my ballot paper at elections. To be a citizen in a democracy is such a privilege and the X on my voting paper is a fundamental element within it.

Anyway, try doing it yourself and see how it will brighten your prayer life. You really will feel a benefit if you concentrate on prayers of thanksgiving for a while. Say one here and now as a test. Notice that you can hardly do so without smiling. So this is a type of prayer which relaxes both your face muscles and your soul muscles. By contrast, prayers in which you express worries and complaints tend to furrow your brow. So, though of course we have the right to bring our anxieties and problems to God, if we are sensible we will not allow ourselves to wallow in them, whereas to wallow in prayers of thanksgiving can do us nothing but good.

What about when life is difficult?
But what about the really bad times of life? Most of us have to go through them. As regular readers of The Plain Truth will know, I went through one myself last year. Paradoxically prayers of thanksgiving can be even more important in the bad times than in the good ones.

Even when life is at its worst, there will always be something for which we can be thankful, perhaps the availability of skilled medical care, or the real blessing which can be provided by the love and support of family and friends, or one of the small comforts provided at home or in hospital, or perhaps a sudden glimpse of some aspect of the beauty of nature.

Being thankful brings strength into our bad times as well as joy into the good ones. When the sky seems totally dark, prayers of thanksgiving can light a little candle which will help us to keep taking one step after another, until the sun rises again.

So even if life is proving difficult, there may still be truth for you in the old hymn – *Count your blessings, count them one by one, and it will surprise you what the Lord has done*. And one final thought. When you are thanking God for whatever blessings you have, don't forget also to say thank you to any people through whom these blessings may have come.

Earlier on I suggested that 'little and large' prayers of thanksgiving could well include basic services like the emptying of our wheelie-bins.

If that seems right to you, why not say a word of thanks not just to God for the team of men who do the emptying but also directly to them? 'Thanks a lot, I really appreciate what you are doing' can be magic words.

In a world which can sometimes seem a rather surly place we really ought to use words like these as much as possible. People are often surprised to hear them. 'Don't mention it,' they sometimes say. But they are usually glad that we have!

📖 PUBLISHED IN THE PLAIN TRUTH: JULY – SEPTEMBER 2006

When life becomes turbulent – here's how to find rest

In April 2014 I had one of the greatest shocks of my life. All seemed normal on Easter Sunday, as I conducted an Easter Communion service in one of our local churches.

The following Tuesday of Easter week I went to see my GP with what I thought was just a case of constipation.

But within an hour I had been admitted to hospital with a diagnosis of bowel cancer!

After a week of assorted tests and treatments, it was arranged that I would go back into hospital in July to have twelve inches removed from my colon.

I am glad to be able to tell you that this operation shows every sign of having been a complete success.

I cannot begin to say how grateful I am to my remarkable surgeon and his team and the sister and ward staff who cared for me afterwards.

This was the NHS at its very best.

A troubled mind

However, from April to July I had to learn to live a day at a time – and sometimes an hour at a time. I did not know whether I would live or die.

My problems were not only physical – my mind and spirit were in turmoil too. Somehow this state of upheaval had to be replaced by a spirit of rest. But how? That was the question.

I found myself thinking of the words of St Augustine, 'Our souls are restless till they find their rest in God.' I remembered the words of Jesus, 'Come to me all you who labour and are heavy-laden and I will give you rest.'[1] I remembered the words from the Letter to the Hebrews, 'There is a rest for the people of God'.[2]

Over the weeks and months that followed, I discovered a six-fold pattern of rest. It had a transforming effect on me. And through this article

I want to share it with you and invite you to store it in your mind. You never know when you may need it.

Step 1

It is my belief that the heart of prayer lies in a state of being in which we quite simply rest in the ESSENCE of God the Father. 'In Him,' we are told, 'we live and move and have our being.'[3] We have no choice about this. If we move a finger a fraction of an inch, we touch God.

On the other hand if we board a space ship and travel to and beyond the boundaries of the known universe, we do not escape him.

Yet there is a choice of sorts. We can rest and rejoice in the God in whose essence we find ourselves. Or we can wriggle and resist and rebel against him. If our choice is to rest and rejoice in our Father, this is a healing process. For as the Bible reminds us, he is not only our Creator but also our Re-creator, 'the Lord who heals'.[4]

Step 2

When we turn our gaze from God the Father to God the Son, it is in his PRESENCE we are invited to rest. During his earthly ministry, Jesus accepted all the limitations of human life.

This meant he was in just one place at a time. But after the Ascension all restrictions of space and time were removed from him. So it is now our privilege to practise his presence, if we so choose.

We have his promise, 'I am with you always, even to the end of the age'[5] and Jesus has not changed. 'He is the same yesterday, today and for ever.'[6] No one ever asked for his healing ministry in vain. He was – and is – infectious with deep healing and his healing power is available for us to discover as we rest in his presence.

Step 3

Turning to God, the Holy Spirit, it is in his ACTIVITY that we are invited to rest.

We can be at rest because the Spirit is at work. In the words of the Epistle to the Ephesians (*Good News Bible Translation*) 'How very great is his power who is at work in us who believe.

This power working in us is the same as the mighty strength which he used when he raised Jesus from the dead.'[7]

If the Holy Spirit works in us we can expect the surge of life in us to strengthen. 'The Spirit of God … will give life to your mortal bodies'.[8] Remember Jesus' promise: 'The Father will give the Holy Spirit to all who ask him.'[9]

Step 4

Then when we have learned to rest in the essence of the Father, the presence of the Son and the activity of the Holy Spirit, our next resting-place should be within the COMMUNION OF SAINTS.

I learned about this in a strange way whilst I was back at home waiting for my bowel cancer operation. One evening our telephone rang and, when my wife answered it, she found the call was from a man who had been present when we had conducted a mission in Northern Ireland back in 2003.

He said, 'You do not know me, but I have a sense that all is not well with you and your husband and so I have found out your telephone number and my wife and I want you to know that we are praying for you.'

In our amazement we felt this was a sign to us from God – but of what? We concluded that we were being invited to rest not just in Father, Son and Holy Spirit but also in the communion of Saints.

In fact a hundred or so cards, letters and messages came to us from near and far. We covered a complete wall in our home with these cards and every time I walked past them, I could feel their healing power touching me. Scripture says, 'There is a rest for the people of God'[10] – I was discovering it day by day.

Step 5

There is also rest to be enjoyed within whatever may be our CLOSEST AND BEST RELATIONSHIP in life.

In my case it was the relationship I have with my wife, Eira. The Bible places great emphasis on marriage. In the book of Genesis the devil's first recorded act is to try to break up the marriage of Adam and Eve.

Jesus himself stresses the importance of marriage. In St Mark's Gospel Chapter 10, verses 6-9 he says that marriage involves a man leaving his parents and joining himself to his wife in a relationship so close that it can be described as a single entity. Christ's term for it is 'one flesh'. He adds this solemn warning. 'That which God has joined together let no one separate.'

To be part of a marriage which provides a strong resting-place is one of life's greatest blessings. But for those who are single or whose marriage has failed or whose marriage-partner has died, there may be a special friendship which can also provide a resting-place.

Scripture tells us, for instance, of the special friendship of David and Jonathan and that when life was difficult Jonathan helped David to find 'strength in God'.[11]

Step 6

Finally, if we are fortunate enough to have GOOD MEDICAL CARE, we can find rest in that also. Ecclesiasticus 38:1 says, 'Honour the medical profession. Medics are God's creation.' And we know that St. Paul was very grateful for the care provided by St Luke, who was a doctor and whom Paul describes as 'the beloved physician'.[12]

You may well have cause to be grateful if you store these six resting places in your memory.

I know by experience how much they meant to me, and now that I have shared them with others, I know that my own experience was not unique.

Shortly after my operation a friend, Geoff, phoned me. He was in a lamentable state, suffering from a terminal lung condition which was causing him and his family great distress.

Though in a permanent state of exhaustion, he could not sleep at night, and both by day and night his sense of darkness and depression were unremitting.

During his telephone call all of this poured out of him. After a time in which I just listened, it seemed right to share my own experience with him and to speak of the six-fold pattern of rest, which had made such a difference to me.

That night he slept deeply and well and when death came to him he was relaxed and at peace. Both his wife and his brother phoned me subsequently to tell me this.

When we are deeply ill, there are only two possible outcomes. We may live. We may die. The miracle of the six resting places which both Geoff and I had come to discover is that they can transform either outcome.

Ultimately, of course, we all will die.

Even Lazarus, whom Jesus brought back from death, eventually went on to die. The thought that came to me, whilst I did not know whether I would live or die myself, is that actually I was in a win-win situation. So are all who put their trust in Jesus and in the Faith he came to bring us.

St Paul expresses this thought superbly in chapter 8 and verses 37-39 of his letter to the Romans. 'We are more than conquerors through Christ who loves us.

For neither death nor life, nor angels, nor principalities, nor powers, nor things present, nor things to come, nor height nor depth – NOTHING IN THE WHOLE OF CREATION will be able to separate us from the love of God, which is in Christ Jesus our Lord.'

📖 PUBLISHED IN THE PLAIN TRUTH: SUMMER – AUTUMN 2015

ENDNOTES

1 Matthew 11:28
2 Hebrews 4:9
3 Acts 17:28
4 Exodus 15:26
5 Matthew 28:20
6 Hebrews 13:8
7 Ephesians 1:19-20
8 Romans 8:11
9 Luke 11:13
10 Hebrews 4:9
11 1 Samuel 23:16
12 Colossians 4:14

Whatever has happened to the BBC?

When I was a young man, it could be taken for granted that the BBC would follow the principles which its first Director General, Lord John Reith, had laid down.

His aims were that the BBC should educate, inform and entertain, but always in a way that was totally wholesome. His principles were embodied in an inscription prominently displayed at the entrance to Broadcasting House, London. It was in Latin, but when it was translated, this is what it said:

'To Almighty God – This shrine of the arts, music and literature is dedicated by the first Governors in the year of our Lord 1931, John Reith being Director General. It is their prayer that good seed sown will produce a good harvest, that everything offensive to decency and hostile to peace will be expelled, and that the nation will incline its ear to those things which are lovely, pure and of good report and thus pursue the path of wisdom and virtue.'

These words have a strange ring in our ears today, because the BBC has changed. It started to happen in the second half of the twentieth century.

The feeling grew that aiming at wholesomeness, decency and virtue was a pretentious and patronising thing to do, and that the aim of the BBC should be not so much to uplift society as to reflect it. The media, it was felt, should be a mirror for the way things are.

What this meant was that if there was a growth in violence in society, it was OK to reflect this on the TV. If bad language was commonplace, programmes could echo it. If there was sexual promiscuity, then the media could and should mirror this behaviour.

If there is a dark side to life these days, then there can properly be a dark side to the TV. Except in the most extreme cases, any form of censorship has come to be regarded as presumptuous and thoroughly out of date.

Promoting a declining society

The problem with looking at things in this way was not immediately seen. Many still do not see it. The trouble is that mere reflection is not possible.

Experience shows that what you reflect you also promote. Reflecting violence promotes violence. Reflecting promiscuity promotes promiscuity. People who hear foul language on the TV are more likely to use it themselves. Reflecting the dark side of things tends to make society darker still.

It sometimes seems that the BBC is a bit like the valley of Siddim in the Bible. In Genesis chapter 14, verse 10 we are told that the valley of Siddim was full of slime pits. The BBC can often seem to be full of slime pits too. When I watch the BBC it is not uncommon for me to feel myself being slimed in the process.

Of course, I know that many programmes are magnificent. *Songs of Praise* is much more than an opportunity to sing along with the telly. It can – and does – introduce us to amazing people doing amazing things with their lives. You can be better for watching and listening.

Some of the nature programmes are also wonderful. The photography can be breathtaking and can help us discover more about creation and the Creator. And some of the quiz programmes are great fun, a source of endless – if not particularly useful – information.

The news programmes keep us informed about world affairs. It is true that they sometimes show an alarming bias of one sort or another, but we have never had such an opportunity to be aware of world events as they happen.

Times have changed

The problem comes when you move to other programmes. There are comedies which seem to be little more than a series of sniggers at the sleazy side of life.

There is an array of films which have never had a lower moral content or more foul language than they do today. Also the BBC's own dramatic productions seem to reflect the notion that nobody will want to watch unless the dark side of life is well to the fore. Things really have changed.

Compare for instance the old and the new versions of *Upstairs Downstairs*. Or see how difficult it is to find a modern equivalent of *Dad's Army* or *Last of the Summer Wine*.

When I used to serve as the TV and Radio Officer for my Diocese, I watched all of this happening and grieved over it. What can we do about it, ordinary folk like you and me?

Well, we can write letters or send emails, because broadcasters are surprisingly influenced by the views of viewers and listeners. We can turn programmes off, because listener/viewer figures really do matter at the BBC, and you are the 'Supreme Controller' of your on/off switch.

We can contact influential people like the Chair of the BBC, or the Prime Minister. They can be contacted either by letter or online, the former at the House of Lords, the latter either at the House of Commons or at 10 Downing Street. We can contact our own MPs. When something strikes us as seriously wrong we can and should point this out with clarity and passion. On the other hand, when something strikes us as really good we can shower praise upon it.

I do believe it is high time that as a nation we looked once again at the Reith philosophy of broadcasting. Reith knew well that there were two ways of looking at broadcasting.

On the one hand, you could make it your aim, he said, 'to carry into the greatest number of homes everything that is best in every department of human knowledge, endeavour and achievement and to avoid whatever might be harmful.'

On the other hand, you could just give people whatever you think they fancy, but the problem with this policy, says Reith, is that 'He who prides himself on giving what the public wants is often creating a fictitious demand for low standards.' Both approaches can get it wrong, but at any rate if you follow the first course you will have aimed high, whereas if you follow the second course and get it wrong you will end up by damaging some people quite unnecessarily.

However, if the Reith philosophy and its embodiment in the inscription at the door of the old Broadcasting House prove too much for our present permissive programme planners to stomach, may I suggest an alternative media motto for their consideration. It consists of just six words:

'ALWAYS COMMUNICATE, SOMETIMES CHALLENGE, NEVER CORRUPT'

If those words or something like them were inscribed near the entrance to New Broadcasting House, and if the BBC started to take them seriously, quite a lot would have to change and half our sleazier programmes might well disappear altogether!

📖 PUBLISHED IN THE PLAIN TRUTH: SUMMER 2012.

PS: Flame Christian & Community Radio now use this as their 'Mission Statement' which is displayed in a frame in their studio.

PPS: Norman Polden, the Station Manager of Flame CCR clearly remembers standing in a field in South Wirral in Autumn 2011, explaining to Roy about the medium wave antenna that Flame was building. Roy was expressing his disgust at the BBC especially in the language used and the moral turpitude the BBC encouraged. One point made by Roy was that the BBC has subtly changed from a mode of reflecting society as it changes, to a mode where the BBC is positively encouraging change within society and has its own agenda in many respects.

Another point Roy made was the way in which what used to be a safety warning at the beginning of a programme that 'this programme may contain scenes of violence/sexual nature/bad language' (warning people they might like to switch off) had now become a stated marketing message encouraging people to actually watch that programme!

And Roy noted that 'strong language' was now a new way of describing what Roy felt was basically 'bad language'. Roy then explained his new, precise media motto 'always communicate, sometimes challenge, never corrupt'.

Norman says that this phrase stuck in his mind and hence the framed sheet in the Flame studio with the Reith statement and Roy's new media motto.

Recently Flame CCR's publicity cards also include the statement:

> *'Our prayer is that we will always communicate,*
> *sometimes challenge and never corrupt....*
> *Roy Lawrence 1931 – 2018.'*

Roy also prayed over their new antenna when we started using it in Autumn 2011. We really appreciated that.

Roy on the radio

On the Wirral Peninsula, where I live, we are fortunate enough to have a local radio station which presents programmes with a distinct Christian slant. Its name is 'Flame'[1] and I am privileged to have been invited to be a director, trustee and broadcaster.

My own contributions are short bursts of Christian teaching in a 'thought for the day' style and can be heard on weekdays, usually at 8.15 in the morning and 5.30 in the afternoon.

Half a million people are able to listen in locally. The station's existence strikes me as a mini-miracle. There are hardly any funds to run it. All the equipment has been either begged, borrowed or bought at a knock-down price.

It broadcasts only by courtesy of a mission church on the outskirts of Birkenhead, which has offered half its premises to the station, and a householder who has allowed the broadcasting aerial to be fixed to a tree in his garden!

The managing director – a remarkable man whose name is Norman Polden – formerly a chartered engineer, somehow offers Wirral a 24-hour broadcasting service, seven days a week, all year round. And although the broadcasters and station staff all work on a voluntary basis, the result is surprisingly professional.[2]

Spectacular results

The station aims to have a healing impact throughout Wirral and beyond and the results are sometimes spectacular.

There was one occasion when someone who had attempted suicide by swallowing a cocktail of pills collapsed to the ground in a coma, pulling a radio off a table as she fell. The radio turned itself on as it hit the floor. The cocktail of pills proved to be not quite fatal and as the coma gradually lifted, the would-be suicide found herself listening to Flame's gospel message. It both changed and saved her life.

Perhaps less spectacular, but no less significant, was an occasion in the life of one of our regular broadcasters. Her name is Laura and she has Multiple Sclerosis. She was brought along to the station after having a fall at home.

Her husband, David, who has a major involvement in Flame felt he could not leave her at home. So he took her with him. Norman's response was to invite her to broadcast and in no time at all she found herself on air. She has become one of Flame's most regular and best loved presenters.

You can hear the effect of her MS upon her voice, but it is this very factor that makes her an inspiration to all who are disabled.

Since Flame began to broadcast, the station has made use of five presenters who suffer from one sort of disability or another.

They include Beryl, Norman's wife, who puts together a splendid programme of assorted hymns every Sunday morning from 9.00 till 11.00. Beryl has made such good progress recently that we may soon have to take her out of the disabled category, but she has been one of a highly significant group.

Let me tell you about Andy. He used to be both mentally and physically ill. He felt he could not leave his own house and if he met others he had real difficulty in talking with them.

However, one day a friend succeeded in persuading him to visit the Flame studio and whilst there Andy revealed an unexpected talent for media work. To everyone's surprise he became a regular broadcaster. This proved the means of reintegrating him into society. It led to his involvement in various forms of community service.

He found the confidence to become a tower guide at Liverpool Cathedral and also to sign on at a local college as a mature student on a course for drama and stage management. In time he was invited to run the college radio service.

Lindsey's story is not dissimilar. She had a problem with drug addiction, but a local Christian couple, Graham and Sue, took her into their home.

Graham had an involvement with Flame, and he took her into the studio. She discovered an aptitude for the technical side of broadcasting and would often 'work the desk', though she always said there was no way in which she would speak into a microphone. However, by accident she found herself doing just that, because when a record came to an end she happened to be the only person in the studio and someone had to introduce the next item of music.

To her surprise she enjoyed it, and so did the listeners. Before long she was a regular presenter and found that simultaneously life began to open up in other ways. She joined the music group in her church and is now in some demand because of a newly found talent as an entertainer.

Flame offered a similar lifeline to Clive. Clive's life was spoilt by a bad stammer. But, strangely, it seemed to vanish if he read poetry. Because he was a talented poet himself he was invited by Norman to host a regular poetry programme on Flame.

His programme became a real joy for listeners, and once again the opportunity offered by Flame opened up the possibility of a new involvement in society. He presents poetry evenings all over Wirral. There is a bonus too.

Unexpectedly his stammer has come under control and he is now able to teach other stammerers how to achieve this control for themselves.

If you wish, you can listen to him and to some of the others I have mentioned, though I am afraid not to Andy, unless an old programme is repeated, because sadly Andy died in his sleep one night not long ago.

If you would like to try the station for yourself, it is not difficult to do so. If you live in Wirral, all you have to do is to tune in to 1521 kHz near the top of your medium wave band.

If you do not live in Wirral, you can still receive Flame providing you have a computer. The station is available all over the world. Just access www.flameradio.org. Towards the top of the display on your screen you will see a long bar bearing the words, 'On-line click to listen on-line.' A single click with your mouse on this bar is all you need to bring you Flame Radio on-line. Have a try!

One final thought. If you should listen in and find you have a comment to make, why not phone the station? Its telephone number is 0151 643 1696. Norman Polden really loves to chat to his listeners.

And, who knows, the next thing you hear on Flame could well be the sound of your own voice!

📖 PUBLISHED IN THE PLAIN TRUTH: AUTUMN 2011

ENDNOTES
1 Flame Christian & Community Radio (CCR) *www.flameradio.org*
2 In 2017, Flame CCR were shortlisted in the Jerusalem Awards in their 'Good Friday' category with *Stations of the Cross: Jesus Dies on the Cross*

PS: Norman Polden, the Station Manager of Flame CCR has this to say about Roy's involvement: 'His contributions of "short bursts of teaching" (we call them "devotionals") are treasured by Flame CCR.

Roy was first introduced to Flame in the winter of 2009 when, with a simple broadcasting desk in the corner of a very large church hall with no heating, Roy would record his devotionals.

From the very beginning Roy had this charming phase 'this is Roy Lawrence, thank you for letting me into your radio'. I liked this phrase so much that all of Roy's talks started in that way.

Within 18 months we were able to offer Roy a comfy

seat in a heated studio. Roy came back regularly with ideas of another series of devotionals.

'Over the years Roy voiced 23 series, some of which were five talks long, others 15. Most of the series were of Roy's invention but I did have the privilege of suggesting topics of: a theologian's view of creation; basic Christianity (the Creed); Calendar (special days for the Church year round); Holy Communion; and the Lord's Prayer.

Roy also suggested that we use talks by Brother David Jardine (Northern Ireland) as well as Dennis Wrigley (Maranatha UK) and obtained permission for us using these talks with Roy introducing them.

'We contacted a few other Christians we knew and were delighted that Howard Simpson, who presents two shows – *Sounds Inspirational* and *Heart and Soul* – on a commercial radio station (HeartlandFM) in Pitlochry, regularly took and used copies of Roy's talks.

This particular article of Roy's talks much of people in the Flame team with disabilities. Roy did not know this, but shortly before he died I too became disabled – an amputee resulting from life-saving surgery after a major cardio-vascular incident.

However I am still able to fulfill my calling to create and further Christian radio in the North West with as my own personal motto: 'I can do all things through Christ who strengthens me', (Philippians 4:13).

The Curse of Political Correctness

S ome people may find this article offensive – perhaps very offensive. For as far as some are concerned, political correctness is a major factor in life. It conditions both their views and their conduct.

Yet I make no apology for it, and the title has been carefully chosen.

For when political correctness comes in through the door, common sense can go out through the window, and so can basic Christian morality.

Those who live by the tenets of political correctness can find themselves enmeshed in a web of notions which reflect no more than the fads and fashions of the time and which have little to do with right and wrong or with the lessons of experience.

Let's look at some examples of political correctness in action.

I have heard of a school where the new headmistress has banned the Christmas Crib. She has explained to her teachers that Christmas Cribs are no longer politically correct. When they asked what they should do with it, she answered, 'Put it in the dustbin.' I am glad to tell you that they refused to do any such thing.

The Red Cross have taken a similar decision. I am told that cribs are no longer allowed to be part of the Christmas decorations in their charity shops. In fact this organization seems hell-bent on de-Christianizing itself. Recently I attended a presentation by one of their speakers in which she explained that the symbol of the cross should be thought of as merely representing the Swiss flag and therefore being a symbol of neutrality. I have to admit that I find myself rather less enthusiastic about the Red Cross than I used to be in the light of their new policy.

Even the word 'Christmas' is regarded as politically incorrect in some circles these days – many preferring 'Season's Greetings' so as not to offend.

Watch out for those words too

Usually the politically correct claim to be liberal and permissive in the language they allow. It is regarded as a sign of narrow-mindedness if you object to obscene or blasphemous language.

So it is that many of the films we see on TV are well laced with the F-word and the like. If there is any warning, we are merely told that the film contains 'strong' or 'adult' language, though I fail to see what is either strong or adult about obscenity and blasphemy.

However, there still is one word which makes the politically correct go positively apoplectic. No penalty is too bad for anyone who happens to use it.

A member of parliament has been condemned and vilified on all sides because whilst talking about the difficulties she envisages in the Brexit process she happened to let the old-fashioned phrase 'the n***** in the woodpile' slip out.

She offered a grovelling apology afterwards, but at the time of the incident in July 2017 it was not accepted. The politically correct are an unforgiving lot and so there is much howling for blood in this case and demands have been made for her resignation as a member of parliament.[1]

I have three large dictionaries and they all contain the phrase she used. These days it is of course outdated and inappropriate. The wise course is not to use it under any circumstances. But can there be any sense of proportion in the blood lust which this incident has produced?
Political correctness often seems to be singularly devoid of a sense of proportion.

Boots the Chemists have found this recently.

The sin which has attracted the wrath of the politically correct is that a representative of the firm had said that it was not their policy to have a pricing policy which would encourage inappropriate sexual conduct.[2]

As I write, I have before me an article from the '*i*' newspaper which says that Boots 'has shown itself to be no better than the Christian-run bakery that refused to ice a cake with the words *Support Gay Marriage*.[3] So speaks the voice of political correctness. Listen and shudder!

Of course we should never subscribe to anything which smacks of any sort of witch-hunt in the case of gay and lesbian people. I guess that, like me, you may well have homosexual friends.

But, having said that, I still cannot feel at ease with the practice, often espoused by those who like to think themselves politically correct, of actively promoting and positively glorifying patterns of sexuality which are far from those which have for centuries ensured the continuation of the human race.

You never know what the latest notion of the politically correct will be. The Mayor of London, Sadiq Khan, has advised that from now on no announcements (on London Underground) should begin with the words 'Ladies and Gentlemen' in case it should offend, and in a bid to make the greetings gender-neutral.

As I said, you never know what the latest notion of the politically correct will be. Perhaps the wisest course would be simply to pay more attention to the observable laws of cause and effect.

One of the effects of doing so would be to see that there is little doubt that the present epidemic of sexually transmitted diseases, with all the problems it causes to the health of the nation and also to the finances of the NHS, is largely caused by the permissiveness which is now rife in society.

Yet it seems that the politically correct thing is never to speak up for traditional morality.

So where should we look?

I must bring this list of illustrations to an end, although I would guess we could all expand it without difficulty.

But if it shows that we cannot safely trust political correctness to be our guiding light, then where on earth can a guiding light be found?

Come with me for a moment to a mountain-top which

is mentioned in the New Testament. There we find Jesus and three of his disciples – Peter, James and John. Mysterious things happened on that mountain-top.

If you want to read the full story you can find it in St Matthew, chapter 17, St Mark, chapter 9 and St Luke, chapter 9, but the final mystery was that a cloud came down on that mountain and out of the cloud came the voice of God the Father. His words were these: 'This is my Son. Listen to him.'

There is a great deal wrong with our world today and that includes our British society. Everybody seems to know that things are not as they should be. The politically correct can certainly see it and are highly vocal in pointing the fact out.

The big question is 'Just what is it that has gone wrong, and what can we do about it?' If we are prepared to take the words of God the Father on the mountain-top seriously, the answer is not too difficult to see. 'This is my Son. Listen to him.'

Our basic problem is – we are not listening to Jesus. The so-called politically correct seem actually to think that they know better than Jesus. They think he is out of date and out of touch. They think that Christianity has failed us.

Listen to the trenchant words of G K Chesterton.[4] 'The Christian ideal has not been tried and found wanting. It has been found difficult and left untried!'

Those who have actually taken Jesus seriously and allowed him to have a pre-eminent place in life come to a very different conclusion.

I remember that when I was young and very raw, I met an older man who shared his secret for fulfilment in life with me. He said 'All through my life I have asked two questions. What would Jesus say? and What would Jesus do?' Those two questions, he said, 'have never ever failed me.'

If we were to take the risk of returning to the simple, searching standards of Jesus, if we were to accept his offer to come into our life and make a difference to us, we would all change and the world would change with us.

Now that I am no longer young but have many years of weather-beaten experience as a vicar behind me, may I share this part of it with you.

I have met many people who have told me they haul behind them a load of all sorts of regrets, but I have never met anyone who said 'I am sorry I put my trust in Jesus.'

In my own life I am more grateful than I can possibly tell you, that as a teenager one day I knelt by my bedside and invited Jesus Christ into my life as my Saviour, Lord and Friend.

You may very well be able to say something similar yourself. But if you haven't, it is never too late to do it!

📖 PUBLISHED IN THE PLAIN TRUTH: WINTER 2017/2018

ENDNOTES

1　On 13 December 2017 it was reported that 'the Conservative MP in Devon who used the N-word has had her suspension lifted. Anne Marie Morris, MP for Newton Abbot since 2010, was given the party whip back yesterday afternoon.' Source: *www.plymouthherald.co.uk/news/local-news/devon-tory-mp-who-used-918411*

2　The article was referring to Boots charging women high rates for the morning after pill because they thought they might use it 'inappropriately' if it's cheap. *www.independent.co.uk/voices/boots-emergency-contraception-morning-after-pill-feminism-women-inequality-inappropriate-a7849521.html*

3　Alice Jones in the '*i*' newspaper, 22nd July 2017.

4　Taken from: *What's Wrong with the World* by G K Chesterton.

PART TWO:
PLAIN TRUTHS ABOUT FAITH

In times of doubt and darkness

Let's face it – it is not always easy to believe in God. Even if you would normally think of yourself as a believer, there are times when you can find yourself wondering whether he exists at all.

There are also times when, even if he does exist, you may be uncertain whether you can really trust him.

Lynn watched her husband, Martin, die from a particularly vicious cancer even though she had prayed long and hard for his healing.

Afterwards she had no answer when her two children asked, 'Why did God let Daddy die?' In fact, when she talked to me about it, she was far from sure that God existed.

Vanessa had a different sort of doubt. After her sister's baby died, though she still felt that life and the universe could not be an accident, she could not bring herself to say her prayers any more. She felt so angry. She told me she hated God!

Gregory had yet another sort of doubt. For him, doubt was an intellectual problem. He was a philosophy student at Oxford and having read books by several atheists whose works were part of his syllabus, he did not know how to refute their arguments and found that the faith he had inherited from his parents was fading away.

How should we react if we find that, for one reason or another, doubt comes to us more easily than faith? May I suggest a few thoughts which may perhaps be helpful? They have been born out of experience of doubt and darkness.

Don't feel guilty

First, if at this moment you should find yourself doubting the existence of God, do be reassured that you don't have to feel guilty about it.

You and I have the right to doubt. That is why God gave us minds. To suppress our minds is not a sign of faith. In fact, it is a sign of the very opposite to faith.

The man whom CS Lewis regarded as his teacher in the Christian Faith, George MacDonald, wrote 'The man that feareth, Lord, to doubt by that fear doubteth thee.'

Many fine Christians have paradoxically found that it was the experience of passing through days of mental and spiritual darkness, which in the end, helped their love of the Lord to grow and mature.

For instance, the Russian novelist, Feodor Dostoievski, whose personal Christianity has been an inspiration to many, wrote, 'My hosanna is born of a furnace of doubt.'

And what if you feel more like Vanessa than Lynn or Gregory?

What if life seems so painful and unfair that you find

yourself nursing anger against God, perhaps even waking up in the middle of the night and shaking a fist at the darkness and demanding to know how a good God can possibly allow so much injustice and suffering?

Again you need not feel guilty. You might be surprised to know how often I have shaken a fist at God, even though I am one of his ministers. You may be even more surprised to find that many of the writers of the Bible have felt just the same way.

Listen, for instance, to the anger in these words from Psalms 44:23-24: 'Wake up Lord! Why are you asleep? Rouse yourself! Don't reject us forever! Why are you hiding from us? Don't forget our sufferings and trouble!'[1]

Or how about these seething prayers of the prophet Jeremiah? 'Why are you like a stranger in our land, like a traveller who stops for one night only?'[2] 'Why do I keep on suffering? Why are my wounds incurable? Do you intend to disappoint me like a stream that goes dry in the summer?'[3]

The Bible teaches that if we have feelings of anger against God, there is no point in suppressing them. God wants our relationship with him to be a real one.

He wants honesty from us, even if this involves an explosion of anger or an admission of a crisis of faith.

However, having said this, although it is right to be honest to God about our negative feelings, yet if we can manage to be at all objective in our thinking, we will know that we are not sufficiently knowledgeable or wise to achieve a total understanding of life.

Our little minds are too small to take in the mystery of the universe. Any God small enough to fit inside my mind would be no God at all.

Where to look

The Christian faith tells us that there is only one way in which we can know about God.

We have to look at Jesus. For Jesus is God's way of presenting himself to us in a way that is comprehensible to the human mind.

And if in any way you and I have seen something of God in the life, ministry and saving love of Jesus, then, when we find ourselves battling with doubt or raging against injustice, the fundamental question to ask is this: 'Is Jesus worth trusting, even in times of doubt and darkness?'

We all end up by trusting somebody or something. We are not meant to go it alone through life. So can you and I think of anyone we can trust more safely than Jesus?

For myself, I know that in all areas where I can test the word of Jesus, it always rings true. So in those areas where I cannot altogether test his word, it seems right and reasonable that I should trust his word.

If doubts and problems still persist, it is no bad thing to remember that Jesus himself had them too! Remember his words on the cross; 'My God, my God, why have you forsaken me?'[4]

Amazingly, although Jesus was God he was allowed to experience the feeling of being God-forsaken. For Jesus experienced human life from the inside.

His own faith, like that of Dostoievski, was fashioned in the furnace of doubt.

Sink or swim

It is, I believe, in this extraordinary man, Jesus Christ, who combines the wisdom of God with a total understanding of human experience, that in times of turmoil our souls can find rest. Sometimes my own prayers are something like this: 'Lord Jesus, just now there are more problems in life than I can cope with, and there are parts of the Christian Faith which I find difficult to believe.

There are so many things I can't fathom, can't see, can't understand. But you can see farther than I can and you have a faith that is greater than mine.

Even when you felt abandoned by the Father, you still prayed to him. Help me to rest in your faith, when my own is running out. You believe in the Father, and I believe in you. You understand more than I do about this mysterious universe and its meaning. I'll rest in your understanding.

Perhaps I can't prove the existence of God the Father, but I trust you and so I'll take him on trust from you. Perhaps I can't understand what he is doing right now; perhaps I feel angry or afraid or both – but I'll hold on to you and trust that you will hold on to me. We'll sink or swim together, Lord. I'd rather sink with you than swim without you. And, come to think of it, Lord, something tells me that whilst your hand is in mine, all cannot be lost.'

Somehow this man, whose fragile body was broken on the cross, is still larger than life, and I know from experience that in his teaching, in his presence, in his love there can be restoration, revitalisation, re-creation when things are at their worst. And we will find that after resting a while with him – perhaps a long while with him – we will find ourselves ready, once again, to take up the challenge of life, to deal with its day-to-day issues, and to pursue the truth, knowing that Jesus has promised 'I am the truth'[5] and that to seek truth is to seek him.

God of the unexpected

One final thought, and it is an enigmatic one: the God and Father of our Lord Jesus Christ is a God of the unexpected. It is a fact of experience that often it is when we reach our lowest point that life yields something that is really worthwhile.

It may be that against all the odds the circumstances of life change. It may be that although circumstances remain the same, yet we find ourselves with a new inner strength, a new ability to cope, a new awareness of God's love.

I have seen this happen in my own life and the lives of many others. St Paul promises that 'in all things God works for good with those who love him',[6] and I am continuously astonished how many people tell me that, in the long run, they have grown and benefited more from the hard times of life than during the easy days.

Maybe in eternity the veil will be lifted from our eyes and God's mysteries will be revealed. In the meantime I believe it is worthwhile to keep faith with Jesus.

In the very day on which I wrote these words, Eddie, a leading member of one of our local churches, told me how much good has come out of it since he and his disabled daughter put her disabilities and all the problems in which they have been involved, into the hands of Jesus.

She is still disabled, but has achieved such interior wholeness that she is continually invited as a speaker to groups who want to learn from her, and, though I don't suppose he knows it, he provides a shining example himself in his local community.

If at this moment you are finding life tough, be honest with yourself and with God, identify both the bad things

and the good things and put the lot in the hand of Jesus.
He hasn't finished with you yet.

So hang on in there – because he's hanging on to you.

📖 PUBLISHED IN THE PLAIN TRUTH: AUGUST – SEPTEMBER 2000.

ENDNOTES

1   Psalm 44:23-24
2   Jeremiah 14:8.
3   Jeremiah 15:18
4   Mark 15:34
5   John 14:6
6   Romans 8:28

Who needs anxiety?

When Bishop Taylor Smith, the notable evangelical churchman who served as Chaplain-General to the forces in World War I, was asked for a contribution to an autograph book, he often used to write this:

The worried cow would have lived till now
If she had saved her breath,
But she feared her hay wouldn't last all day
And she mooed herself to death!

I am told that the word 'worry' comes from an Anglo-Saxon word meaning 'wolf'. Certainly worry can be like a wolf in the way it tears at life – not that it tears the troubles from tomorrow. What it does is to tear the strength and peace from today.

Anxiety is useless, dangerous and very common. Our age has been called 'the age of anxiety'. So if the Christian Church has a Gospel for today, a Gospel which heals, it must be seen to speak relevantly and effectively to the many folk who are fettered by anxiety.

There are two types of anxiety.

First, there is anxiety about a specific object. Bishop Taylor Smith's worried cow knew what she was worrying about and so do many anxious men and women. 'Will I get the job I want?' 'Will I pass my exam?' 'Will I be alright when I go into hospital?' 'Are my children alright, now they are living away from home?' And so on.

Secondly, there is another sort of anxiety – a deeper sort – that does not seem to have a specific object at all. 'Milly' comes into my mind. She is a natural worrier. She has to have something to worry about. If there is no handy problem around, she will invent something, because the worry is deep inside her.

I think of 'Poppy' who, because she is deep down anxious, cannot bear to be ignored. She has to be the centre of attention.

At first glance she looks self-confident, but those who know her well can see that behind the attention-seeking there is deep anxiety which means she cannot face being really alone.

Then there is 'Alexander' who is afraid of deep friendships, afraid of being hurt and so always keeps his distance.

He looks self-sufficient, but underneath it all he is not secure enough to trust another person. One day, his self-sufficiency may crack, and if that happens he will be in for a nervous breakdown.

Deep insecurity is common, commoner than one might think, because we do not like to admit it and so we try to hide it, even from ourselves. But of course, hiding something does not make it go away. The anxiety lurks under the surface and affects our behaviour in strange and painful ways.

How can God help?

How specifically can the healing power of Christ be brought to bear on an anxiety condition?

Anxiety about something specific, though it can be agonising, is the easier sort to deal with. The rule of thumb that my wife and I worked out when our younger son was very seriously ill as a baby was: do your best, and leave the rest to God.

In our case, this meant taking the best practical action humanly possible, but at the same time putting the whole situation, including the ultimate outcome, in the hands of God.

It was a philosophy that made a healing difference. We managed to cope with one day at a time and, as for each tomorrow, we reminded ourselves that the God who stands beyond time and space was already there and that the future was best left in his caring hands.

But what about when there is no external circumstance which we can commit to him – just an inner emptiness? This sort of anxiety can dominate and ruin life.

How does the Christian Faith offer healing here? I believe there is a basic threefold truth, which we need to appropriate for ourselves:

God made me

He made me and no creation of his is valueless

God loves me

He loves me even to the point of the cross

God wants me

He wants me and he has something for me to do and to be in his service

I have watched these truths having a healing impact in my own life and in the lives of many others too.

The healing usually happens gradually, but it happens inexorably and lastingly, once these convictions have taken root in the ground of our being.

If it should be that you are a natural worrier, then test-drive these three truths. Take them into your prayers. Every morning and every evening, when you say your prayers, say to yourself slowly and deliberately: *God made me*, and he is a skilled creator who does not make rubbish. *God loves me;* he would have sent his son to die for me if I had been the only person in the world!

And *God wants me*; he has something for me to do and to be which is absolutely unique. If I fail to do it and be it, part of God's eternal purpose will be eternally unfulfilled!

Of course I am a sinner, but I am a precious sinner, a forgiven sinner if my trust is in Jesus.

So I have better things to do with my time than to squander it on anxieties that Jesus has actually *commanded* me to lay aside.

So, why worry?

We started with a poem. Here is another. It is by Elizabeth Cheney and you may well know it already:

Said the Robin to the Sparrow, 'I would really like to know, why these anxious human beings rush around and worry so.'

Said the Sparrow to the Robin, 'Friend, I think that it must be, that they have no heavenly Father such as cares for you and me.'

But of course, we do have a heavenly Father and Jesus is absolutely determined that we should know it.

In the 'Sermon on the Mount', he recognises a range of things that people fuss and fret about: cash, clothing, cuisine, and all sorts of coming events. About it all he asks, 'Why worry?'

He gives us this overriding principle: 'Be concerned above everything else with the kingdom of God and with what he requires of you and he will provide you with all these other things, *so do not worry.*'[1]

St Paul assures us that there is absolutely nothing either around us or within us that should make us captives to anxiety.

The reason is that the peace of God is more powerful than any perils that may beset us. 'God's peace,' he says, 'which is far beyond human understanding will keep your hearts and minds safe in union with Christ Jesus.'[2] St John puts it even more simply: 'God is love.'[3]

So, to go back to the title of this article, 'Who needs anxiety?'

The answer, which Jesus gives to all that put their trust in him, is: '*You* certainly don't!'

Too simplistic

I know that nothing ever seems as simple as that in this complicated world.

In the short term, there is good news in the fact that whilst our anxieties are still part of us, God can use them to make us less rigidly selfish and more sympathetic to others who have similar anxieties.

But in the longer run, the Bible leaves us in no doubt that it remains God's will to loose us from every fear.

In the unforgettable words of St Paul's letter to the Romans, chapter 8, verses 38-39, you and I are called to know with total certainty that 'there is nothing in death or life, in the realm of spirits or superhuman powers, in the world as it is or the world as it shall be, in the forces of the universe, in the heights or depths, *nothing in all creation* that can separate us from the love of God in Christ Jesus our Lord'.

📖 PUBLISHED IN THE PLAIN TRUTH: OCTOBER – NOVEMBER 2001.

ENDNOTES

1   Matthew 6:33-34.
2   Philippians 4:7
3   1 John 4:8

Is guilt a problem?
Four texts from the Bible that could change your life!

Recently The Plain Truth received a moving letter from Mr Victor R. of Bedfordshire. This is what he wrote: 'I thought I would have to carry my sins to eternity, but I find I might have a chance after all. Are there any scriptures I can turn to, to help me through?'

It is so good to make it plain that the Christian faith answers Victor's question with a resounding 'Yes!' One of the principal purposes of the Bible is to bring hope and help to those who are sinners – and know it.

Congratulations
Surprisingly, the first word which Christianity speaks to those who are burdened with a personal sense of sin is **'Congratulations!'** For the sinner who has significant insight to be aware that he or she has broken God's laws

has already taken the first step towards finding a solution. That person can see further and better than many others.

In fact, it is a characteristic of the mega-sinners of this world that they often have so sense of sin at all.

We are told that Harold Shipman had no sense of guilt or remorse and that the same was true of both Al Capone and Adolf Hitler.

So my first scripture for Victor – and for all of us – is 1 John 1:8 'If we say we have no sin, we deceive ourselves and the truth is not in us.'

Victor is to be congratulated on not deceiving himself. Can the same be said of you and me? For everybody in this flawed world breaks God's laws, but not everybody knows it.

Listen

The second word which the Christian faith says to us if we are burdened with a sense of sin is '**Listen**' – listen to the good news of the Gospel; for the Gospel could hardly be better news.

At this moment, God the Father is saying to every repentant sinner, 'My Son, Jesus, has lived among you; died for you; risen from the dead and ascended into heaven, just so that he can be available to you here and now. Because of him you do not have to bear your sins alone. He bears them with you – and for you.' Sin's deadly power need never again have the last word in life. Out of the many scriptures which make this promise, we could do no better than to select John 3:16 'God so loved the world that he gave his only begotten Son, that whosoever believes in him should not perish but have everlasting life.'

Respond

The third word is '**Respond**'. For Jesus has done almost everything to make it possible for you and me to be forgiven and restored to the place which God wants us to have in his kingdom – almost, but not quite, everything.

There still remains one thing for us to do because God respects our freedom and never forces his will or his love upon us, and so he does not force his Son upon us.

You and I have to say 'yes' to Jesus. We have to invite him into our lives, and our third text comes from Revelation 3:20 which pictures Jesus waiting courteously for permission to come into our lives and saying these words: 'Behold, I stand at the door and knock. If anyone hears my voice and opens the door, I will come in.'

There is a prayer of response which I have shared with thousands of people during my years in ministry. If you have never said one like it, it is important to do so here and now:

Jesus, I know I am a sinner, but I also know that you love me and gave yourself for me. You offer to come into my life if I will let you in. You offer healing for the sins and hurts of my soul. You offer to feed me with your own truth. Gratefully I accept your offer to be my Saviour, Lord and friend. I put my trust in you and want you to work in me, healing me, feeding me, living in me. Help me to use my life in your service. Thank you for all you are going to do in me. Amen.'

Expositions of the Gospel usually take us through the three stages represented by the three words and the three texts quoted so far, and the Bible tells us that there is joy in heaven every time a sinner hears this good news and makes a personal prayer of response.

So my reply to Victor could easily end here. But, on this occasion, I want to add a fourth word and a fourth text, for they add something which we often forget, though I believe it is dear to the heart of God.

Enjoy

The fourth word is '**Enjoy**'. Have you ever noticed that if you go out to a restaurant for a meal, very often after the menu has been studied and the meal has been selected, cooked and served, the waiter will say the word 'enjoy' before he leaves your table?

It is the same with the Gospel banquet. When a repentant sinner has heard and responded to the Christian message, God will be disappointed if the joys of the Gospel are not experienced and savoured to the full.

Our fourth text comes from John 10:10. In it Jesus says of his disciples, 'I have come that they may have life, and have it *abundantly*.' That's how God wants it to be for Victor and for us all.

So, I wonder, have you and I claimed the joys and benefits of the Gospel to the full? There is such a wide range of them. For instance, how about this as an example:

I will remember Jasmine, a lady who for years had endured a cumbersome surgical collar and was often in pain. She asked me if I would visit her in her home and as we talked she was moved to tell me of sin she had committed many years before.

'Every night,' she said, 'before I go to sleep, I plead with God for forgiveness for that sin.'

It gave me real pleasure to be able to tell her the good news about God's gift of forgiveness through Jesus Christ and to offer this prayer prescription for her: 'Tonight, before you go to sleep, ask once more for forgiveness, but do so quite specifically in the name of Jesus, who died on the cross to be your Saviour and to bring you forgiveness fully, freely and forever.

'Then tomorrow don't ask for forgiveness for that sin again. If you feel you must mention it, just say: "Thank you God, for forgiving me my sin." And the next night and the night after, and as long as you think it necessary, just say, "Thank you God that you have forgiven me through Jesus Christ."'

Within two weeks, Jasmine had discarded her surgical collar and was free from pain. It had taken its leave along with her guilt and stress.

Full impact

We should never experience the Gospel with the top two inches of our mind. It should have an impact on our whole being, body, mind and spirit – all that we are, all that we feel and all that we do. It should influence our health and happiness, our attitudes and relationships, our total quality of life.

I am grateful to Victor for giving me this opportunity to say this, and I hope he finds the four words – congratulations, listen, respond and enjoy – and the four texts that go with them truly liberating.

The four texts are all from the writings of St John, but I could just as easily have chosen texts from St Paul or the other Gospel writers, or from elsewhere in the Scriptures. For the Bible is a book about the great love in God's heart and the great plans he has for each one of us.

It is true that it also warns us about the perils of breaking God's laws, but that is not in order to fixate us upon our faults and failures; it is that we may marvel at the immensity of the saving work which is the heart of the Christian faith and know that those who hold fast to Jesus need never be without joy that comes from his presence here or in eternity.

Just one final thought to round this all off.

It comes from John Bunyan's great book, *The Pilgrim's Progress*. Many people know that in Bunyan's story when Christian comes to the foot of the cross, the heavy burden of guilt which he carries becomes dislodged: 'His burden loosed from off his shoulders and fell off his back and began to tumble and continued to do so, till it came to the sepulchre, where it fell in, and I saw it no more.'

But that's not the end of Bunyan's description. Don't miss the sentences that follow. Then, we are told: 'Christian was glad and lightsome.' He 'gave three leaps for joy'. And he went on his way singing!

How's that for liberation?

📖 PUBLISHED IN THE PLAIN TRUTH: APRIL – MAY 2004.

Anything to declare?
The place of confession in prayer

In the June edition of The Plain Truth I offered you some thoughts about adoring and praising God. Adoration is the first of the four traditional elements which should feature in our daily prayers. The other three are Confession, Thanksgiving, and Supplication. We can easily remember these four ingredients because their first letters spell out the word ACTS.

In this article may I invite you to consider the second of these ingredients – Confession? It is not one which we necessarily fancy, because we think it is a type of prayer that will probably make us miserable. But in point of fact the very opposite is true. Confession is actually a step along the road to joy!

The heart of confession lies in bringing the 'real me' to God without self-deception or self-justification.

It says, 'Here I am, Lord, warts and all,' or, in the words of the famous hymn, 'Just as I am, I come.' It involves admitting to ourselves the things which are wrong in our lives, coming clean to God about it, saying sorry and asking forgiveness.

Most people find it helpful to have a systematic procedure which can be used from time to time in self-examination and there are passages in the Bible which can be used in this way as a checklist.

An obvious example is that of the Ten Commandments. You can find them in Exodus 20:1–17, or at the beginning of the Communion Service in the *Prayer Book*.

The best way to use them is not only to think about their literal meaning, but also about the issues which each raises.

So, for instance, when we consider the second commandment, 'Thou shalt not make to thyself any graven image,' we ought not just to congratulate ourselves on not having erected a golden calf in our back garden, but we should take time to consider the wider question: 'Are there any things or people that I have made into idols by behaving as though they were more important than God? Money? Popularity? Possessions? Power? A private sin? Respectability? Pleasure? Myself? My family? Some other person?'

Or again, when we come to the eighth commandment, 'Thou shalt not steal,' we should not only consider the question of whether or not we are absolutely financially honest (though that in itself will catch most of us out), but we should also ask ourselves questions like, 'Have I stolen praise or credit that does not belong to me? Have 1 stolen a chance or opportunity that ought by rights to have been someone else's? Have I stolen time from my employer?'

Or, by contrast, 'Have I stolen time as an employer by not being fair to any who work for me? At home have I been guilty of stealing love from my children because I have been too busy or tired or selfish to bother with them? Have I stolen from society by adopting a 'take-all and give-nothing' style of life? Have I stolen from God himself, because, though all I have comes from him, I offer so little of my time, my energy and my possessions back to him?'

The love test

Or if you would like an alternative to the Ten Commandments, how about St. Paul's famous chapter which deals with Christian love, the one that contains the words, 'Love is very patient, very kind. Love knows no jealousy'... and so on?[1] We can turn it into a series of questions and can find it a useful aid to confession, if we apply it to ourselves – 'Am I very patient? Am I very kind? Do I know no jealousy? Do I make no parade and give myself no airs? Am I never rude, never selfish, never irritated, never resentful? Am I never glad when others go wrong? Am I gladdened by goodness? Am I always eager to believe the best? Always hopeful? Always patient?'

The point of asking ourselves questions like these and of having the courage to stay around for an answer, is that it enables us to bring an awareness of our sins to God and to ask for forgiveness, relying as we do so on the Biblical assurance that 'If we say we have no sin, we deceive ourselves and the truth is not in us, but if we confess our sins, God is faithful and just and will forgive us our sins and cleanse us from all unrighteousness.'[2] We will not only feel better for the knowledge of God's forgiveness, but the improvement of our relationship with him will begin to make a positive difference to the sort of people we are.

Jesus died upon the cross for our forgiveness, but his sacrifice will be wasted, if we refuse to acknowledge our own personal need to be forgiven.

Not just our sins

An article on confession could easily end at this point. However, owning up to our sins is only one element in the prayer of confession.

There are at least two more which are often forgotten. In prayers of confession we are called to come to God not just with an awareness of our sins, but also an awareness of our disabilities – emotional, spiritual and physical.

These may not be our fault at all, but they will constitute a basic fact about our nature. For example, one of the commonest emotional disabilities is a feeling of insecurity and fearfulness. It can lie beneath the surface of life and exercise a paralysing effect on all we are and all we do.

Its origin can go back to our very earliest years. It may well be painful to acknowledge it, but if we allow ourselves to bring this or any other disability to God, we can then ask Jesus to meet us at our point of need.

We will never ask this in vain. He is the Saviour who loves to say, 'Yes'. If it is a spirit of fearfulness that we bring to him, what he will do is to flood it and us with his love.

This will make a fundamental difference because 'perfect love casts out fear',[3] even if it involves a long-term healing process.

Speaking personally, one of the joys of my own life has been to experience the way in which Jesus has gradually lifted the burden of anxiety and fearfulness which for many years was part of my experience of life and which caused me particular grief when I was a little boy.

Confess your success too

Our thoughts about the prayer of confession have so far concentrated on the negative side of life. However if we leave the subject there, we will miss a thought of supreme importance.

In times of confession we are called not just to bring our sins and disabilities to God, but also our positivities and our potential, for these too are essential parts of our reality.

I do hope you know what a truly special person you are. You exist because God made you – and he does not create rubbish. And the human life that he has invested in you is so precious to God that he has actually shared it himself.

That is the central truth which we celebrate every Christmas and we must never allow the celebratory trimmings to make us forget the real reason for this season.

Human nature has of course gone badly astray, but that has not led God to abandon us. We are precious enough for God to seek to redeem us. The cross of Jesus not only tells us how terrible human sinfulness is; it also tells us how much God values and loves us.

And God has something for you and for me to do and to be, something of deep significance, both here on earth and then within the mystery of eternity.

The Gospel teaches us that God has it within his amazing mind and his generous heart for you and for me to evolve into shining miracles of glory, if only we will allow him to have his way with us.

We cannot at present conceive that which we are meant to become, and yet there are tantalizing hints in scripture and, just occasionally, tantalizing glimpses within our own spiritual life. To know and acknowledge this is a vital part of the prayer of confession.

So then, confession involves admitting and repenting our sins, so that we may receive God's forgiveness.

It involves acknowledging our disabilities, so that, as we practise the presence of Christ, he may meet us at our deepest points of need with his own loving, life-changing power.

And it involves recognising our value and our potential so that, as we do so, God may help us further along the way to our destiny.

It is all a million miles away from the grovelling, self-contemptuous exercise which some people confuse with the prayer of confession.

One final point

We may need some help in this important area of prayer. Some churches recommend that the confession of sin should take place in the presence of a priest or minister, and all churches make provision for this if it is felt to be helpful. The whole procedure is of course totally confidential. Also, if we are to explore the painful inner areas which can underlie our experiences of disability, it can be helpful to seek the guidance of a wise, Christian counsellor or a trained listener.

We are not meant to be alone on our prayer journey. Some find it helpful to have a 'soul friend' with whom life's issues can be discussed. But these are matters for every individual to decide personally.

The important thing is to know that, whether in private prayer or in the context of Christian ministry and friendship, we are privileged to open our heart to a listening God.

To be 'honest to God' is never a non-event. That is the heart of confession and we neglect it at our cost.

📖 PUBLISHED IN THE PLAIN TRUTH: DECEMBER 2004 – JANUARY 2005

ENDNOTES

1　1 Corinthians 13:4-7
2　1 John 1:8-9
3　1 John 4:18

Dark night of the soul

Recently I have passed through six of the most extraordinary weeks in my whole life.

It all began when I went into hospital for an eye operation. This was a delicate procedure and it had to be followed by ten days during which I was required to remain in a face-down position.

But I went in with high hopes. Literally hundreds of people had promised that they would pray for me. We covered a complete wall in our home with their cards and messages. So I expected that I would feel supported by their prayers and that all would go well.

How wrong you can sometimes be!

The first night spent lying face downwards stirred up an old back problem. So that was a pain – quite literally so.

Then on the second day I started with a totally unexpected attack of shingles of the head, which was made all the worse by the fact that initially nobody in the hospital would take it seriously. Then my waterworks became completely blocked, a problem soon aggravated by a condition known as haematuria, in which urine becomes blood-red – this eventually required a second operation.

In all, I had to be admitted to hospital three times during the course of those six weeks.

However, my worst experience was not a physical one at all. In addition to the original operation, the shingles and the waterworks blockage I found myself assailed by a spiritual problem of soul-shattering dimensions.

Suddenly and unaccountably all my faith deserted me. I found myself in a state of complete spiritual darkness. All awareness of the presence of God was taken from me. The only scriptural text which had any reality for me was 'My God, my God, why have you forsaken me?'[1]

In fact the very concept of God now seemed alien to me. Suddenly my whole life and ministry seemed a fraud, a pointless and empty concoction of one delusion after another.

All the services I had ever led, all the sermons I had ever preached, all the books and articles I had ever written – all of this and much more now seemed a ghastly exercise in deception. I felt I had deceived myself and everyone else.

In the annals of Christian devotional theology there is a name for what I was experiencing. It is known as the 'Dark Night of the Soul.' St John of the Cross and other Christian mystics have written about it in some detail. In the *New Dictionary of Pastoral Studies* (SPCK) Archbishop Rowan Williams describes it as a state in which '…the very thought of God makes no sense whatsoever and one's sense or security and self-worth seems to disappear. This is when darkness reaches right into the depths of the spirit.'

In theory this was a phenomenon about which I knew well. I had been told about it at Theological College. I knew that some of the greatest saints had experienced it; And I knew in fact that to undergo it is in some ways regarded as a privilege.

However this knowledge was of no use to me whatsoever. It was, I think, the worst fortnight of my life, and my wife, Eira, to whom I poured out all these feelings, said it was the worst fortnight of hers too.

The anguish of this experience defies both understanding and description. Whilst within it I found myself totally unable to help myself. However, having said that, there were some factors in the situation which were helpful.

Even though I no longer believed in God or in prayer, yet it was strangely good to know that so many people were praying for me. I felt that at a purely human level it was better to have good and caring thoughts projected towards me than to be without them.

Also perversely I could not stop talking to the God in whom I no longer believed. I poured out my sense of anger and abandonment onto whatever there might be behind the God who was now non-existent as far as I was concerned.

And there were people who allowed me the privilege of doing the same thing to them, people who found time just to listen. I shall never cease to be grateful to three listeners who gave me the hospitality of their time and attention in a totally non-judgemental way.

One was my wife, Eira, and the other two were the hospital chaplain and a wonderful night nurse, who spent an hour with me at a time when my spiritual darkness was deepest.

Ultimately I managed to claw my way out of that place of horror and back to a sort of faith. It was a slow and agonizing process and involved rediscovering some of the basic reasons why many years ago as a teenager I started to be a committed Christian.

By the time I went into hospital for my second operation, the dark night experience had become a thing of the past. By then a sense of the presence, the peace and the protection of God had come back to me. I now felt supported physically, emotionally and spiritually. Darkness had now been replaced by light, and I found it almost impossible to pray in any other mode than that of thanksgiving.

Most readers are probably finding this article very puzzling because I guess that the great majority of Christians have no personal experience to compare with it.

If this is true of you, then God bless you and shield you from ever having to explore it at a personal level. However, it may well be that for just a few, the things I have written will be frighteningly familiar and to some of you they will become so at some point in the future.

So it has been suggested to me by various people whose opinions I value that I should write about this experience whilst the anguish of it is still fresh in my mind and soul.

Here then, for what they may be worth, are a handful of thoughts and conclusions for you to consider. It is not easy to find adequate words to express them. St John of the Cross clearly struggles with his own powers of description and comprehension when he writes, 'what the sorrowful soul feels most in this condition is its clear perception, as it thinks, that God has abandoned it and in his abhorrence of it has flung it into darkness.' He says, 'the soul feels very keenly the shadow of death and the pains of hell' and that 'it is so with it for ever.'

These words which used to sound so strange to me now have a terrible resonance.

The Dark Night is like nothing else in the whole of mental and spiritual experience. It is neither a state of intellectual difficulty blocking the way to belief, nor is it a form of emotional depression. It is a sort of vision and yet it is the very opposite of what we generally mean by a vision.

Usually we think of a vision as having a positive content, as in the case of a vision of God, or vision of light or a vision of our calling in life.

But here, by contrast, is a vision of darkness, a vision of godlessness, of dereliction and desolation, of emptiness and purposelessness.

Why a good God should allow it is beyond understanding, whilst it endures. Yet, as I now look back upon it, I can see, just as St John of the Cross did, that many positive things can be said about it.

John sees it in terms of purgation. He writes that it is not 'till the spirit is humbled, softened and purified and grows keen and delicate and pure that it can become one with the Spirit of God, according to the degree of union of love which his mercy is pleased to grant it.'

What then are my own positive perceptions about this experience? I am a firm believer both in the power of prayer and in the Church's calling to exercise the ministry of Christian Healing. But it has always been my conviction that we must never be glib about either of these things. That conviction has been deepened and strengthened by my experience of the dark night of the soul.

Before I went into hospital a clergyman of my acquaintance patted me on the shoulder and said, 'Don't worry, you'll have no problems. Everything will be just fine. I know it.'

Of course, he knew no such thing! This sort of glibness is a betrayal both of life's reality and of gospel truth. False comfort is no comfort. God save us from glib clerics. They are as of little use as glib politicians.

Yet, having said that, there is a real sense in which even really bad things can have good consequences for us if we have anything of the love of God in us.

St Paul teaches this very strongly. He writes, 'In all things God works for the good of those who love him'.[2] I think I would have hit anyone who said that to me whilst I was deep within the darkness. Yet I can now bear witness that even in that dreadful place the healing power of God can be at work.

When I emerged from it I discovered that a number of profound inner fears and temptations, things with which I had wrestled for many years, seemed no longer to have a place in me. Mysteriously I had been moved on in my spiritual journey.

Also, I am now doubly sure of the importance of many of life's positive things. I learned afresh just how precious real practical help can be when life is at its most difficult.

Friends and neighbours who made themselves freely available to us were such a blessing, I saw new depth and

meaning in the old rhyme from Adam Lindsay Gordon:
> *'Life is mainly froth and bubble, two things stand like stone, kindness in another's trouble, courage in your own.'*

Indeed I found new depth and meaning in many things. Perhaps, before I end these thoughts, I may share just a couple of them with you.

My time of spiritual darkness happened to coincide with the end of Lent, and I found that Holy Week had an extraordinary personal relevance for me; Good Friday came to life for me in a particularly unique way.

Till then I was not free from pain, but on Good Friday the pain ceased. To me it seemed that Christ had taken my own pain into himself as he hung upon the cross. The text 'By his wounds you have been healed'[3] had never seemed so literally true.

Also, the day after Good Friday, sometimes known as 'Holy Saturday', has come to have a new significance for me. It is the day when we consider the doctrine of Christ's descent into hell.[4]

This has never meant much to me in the past, but, because experiencing the dark night of the soul can seem rather like being in hell, suddenly it was very important to believe that, when I had no means of finding Jesus in the darkness, he could still find me. And indeed it proved to be true that from Holy Saturday onwards, as Lent turned into Easter, faith gradually returned to me.

As I struggled out of that state of dereliction, increasingly I saw that no matter how deep and dense spiritual darkness may be, ultimately it cannot resist the light of Christ.

I should have known it, of course, from the mighty prologue of St John's Gospel which assures us that whenever the light of Christ has invaded the darkness which is all too characteristic of our world then, in the words of the Good News Bible, 'the darkness has never put it out!'

📖 PUBLISHED IN THE JULY – SEPTEMBER 2005 ISSUE OF THE PLAIN TRUTH

ENDNOTES

1 Psalm 22:1; Mark 15:34
2 Romans 8:28
3 1 Peter 2:24
4 1 Peter 3:19

Sin makes you stupid!

It is a major theme of the Wisdom Literature in the Bible that God gave us common sense in order that we might use it and that, as we do so, we and the world might benefit from it.

It is a further theme of this literature that the closer we keep to God the better will be our capacity to see things clearly and do things well. In the well-known words from the Book of Proverbs, 'The fear of the Lord is the beginning of wisdom'.[1]

There is nothing new or unusual in this thought, but what we do not always remember is that a concept, like a coin, has two sides to it.

If the fear of the Lord is the beginning of wisdom, it must also be true that turning away from God will involve a weakening of common sense and a loss of the capacity for straight thought and clear vision. In other words – sin makes you stupid. It is easy to forget this and to fall for the devil's disinformation service, when he tells us that godliness is a mark of the dull-minded, whereas sin is really rather smart. But it is not without reason that Jesus tells us the devil is a liar[2] and it takes only a little thought to see that if we can manage to resist those fads and fashions in society which lead us away from God, we shall do ourselves a very real favour.

Let's look at some illustrations.

I have to admit that I enjoy a glass or two of good wine, particularly along with a special meal. So did Jesus.[3]

But abusing alcohol should be nobody's idea of a good time. The description of a hangover in the book of Proverbs, chapter 23 is an absolute classic:

'Who's got trouble? Who's got misery? Who gets bad-tempered and quarrelsome? Who gets bruises without knowing why? Who gets bloodshot eyes? The pub-crawler who spends hours swilling one drink after another!
Don't let the sparkle and smooth taste of strong drink deceive you. In the end it bites like a snake and is as venomous as a cobra.

Your eyes will play you tricks. Your speech will be confused. You will feel like a man tossing out at sea, swaying about at the top of a ship's mast.

You will feel like someone who has been beaten up without even knowing what has happened. Yet next day you'll go on drinking and it will all happen again!'[4]

Being a lager-lout or a lager-ladette, or any other sort of alcohol abuser makes absolutely no sense. But our sins never do, not if we can manage to think straight.

Ruined lives

This is certainly true of the sexual sins. If the world were to accept the simple searching standards of Jesus, the present global epidemic of sexually transmitted disease would soon begin to relax its sinister grip. Our own country suffers in very many ways as a result of the permissiveness which is so fashionable.

Even those who reject that permissiveness suffer, not least because so many of the resources of the National Health Service are absorbed by sexual diseases that there is less available for everyone else.

There are many other ways too in which the sexually promiscuous involve those who aren't. I think of a lovely young Christian girl who came to me for ministry, whose life had been spoiled by congenital syphilis and another whose life had been spoiled by the abuse she had suffered at the hands of her father. Or at a global level, think of the millions of innocent AIDS-babies in Africa.

The trenchant advice of St Paul is 'Avoid sexual looseness like the plague!'[5] 'Avoid practising it. Avoid talking about it. Avoid slavering over it. Live your lives in love – the same sort of love which Christ gives us. But, as for sexual immorality in all its forms – don't even talk about such things... For of this you can be quite certain, that neither the immoral nor the dirty-minded man... has any inheritance in the kingdom of Christ and of God. Don't let anyone fool you on this point, however plausible his argument.'[6]

We would know that this advice makes sense, if our perspective had not been distorted by the sins of society.

All in the mind

However let's move away from the physical sins and think for a moment about those of mind and attitude, which can be even more dangerous.

For instance hate and prejudice will wither our souls from within, if we give way to them, as well as splintering and damaging society.

There are so many instances of this in recent history, whether we think of the anti-Semitism of Nazi Germany or the brutalities of apartheid South Africa or the cruelty of the Ku Klux Klan in America or the horrendous persecution of Christians around the world today by extremist regimes of one sort or another.

Under such circumstances nobody wins, everybody loses. Even humdrum grudges are not without their dangers. We tend to cuddle our grudges as though they were precious, but if we can clear our minds for a moment, it is evident that they damage us.

If I am in the grip of a grudge, I lose my capacity for enjoying life. My sleep may be interrupted. My food may not taste as good. In a strange way I will find myself in the power of the person against whom the grudge is held, because when I come across that person, my stomach may go into a knot, my blood pressure may go up. My freedom will be diminished.

In other words, I would do myself a clear favour by letting my grudges go. Why is it that so often I fail to see this? Because my sins make me stupid. They close my eyes and dull my mind.

The best policy?

One further illustration. There is a lot of dishonesty in society. Yet honesty really is the best policy. Truthfulness is simpler and better than deceit, because truth is self-consistent, whereas in the words of Sir Walter Scott, 'Oh, what a tangled web we weave, when first we practise to deceive'. Dishonesty is also beset with pitfalls at a financial level. Society is certainly the worse for it. All prices are substantially higher to compensate for pilfering in shops and stores and for expensive security systems. We all pay extra taxes to keep the prisons going. The general quality of life is diminished if people cannot feel safe either on the street or in their own homes.

Moreover the dishonest do themselves no favours. They never know when they may be caught, and even if they are not, the words of Jesus still ring true across the centuries 'What shall it profit a man if he shall gain the whole world and lose his own soul?'[7]

I shall never forget going to a watch-repairer in a little back-street shop when I was a student. He charged me just six old pence for repairing my watch. When I said, 'That's not much,' he replied, 'It's all the job was worth.'

When I pointed out that I would never have known that, he just said, 'Well, I would, and I'm the one who has to live with myself.' He probably never became wealthy and yet in a real sense he was rich indeed, and he taught me that we can surrender our personal integrity much too easily and much too cheaply.

So where do these thoughts lead us?

In Britain the feel-good factor in life leaves a lot to be desired these days. We need something of a lift, and there is quite a lobby of those who urge that greater permissiveness would give us that lift.

But if we can manage to think straight, there is little evidence that they are right and lots of evidence that they are wrong.

The Bible takes precisely the opposite view. It says that if society is to have any sort of real lift, there will first have to be a rediscovery of values. Or to put this in the traditional language of the Book of Proverbs: 'Righteousness exalts a nation'.[8]

The Christian faith teaches that it is precisely because God is a caring Father that he gives us standards by which to live – and not only standards but his own Son also to be our companion along life's way.

There are so many reasons for opening our eyes to God's standards and God's Son, but surely there are no reasons at all for keeping our eyes firmly shut.

We may not fancy admitting that our society has got so many things wrong. We may fancy even less admitting that we have done so personally.

But we can take heart.

If we give God a chance he will work for us, with us and in us. Christ has lived and died to bring us new life. As St Paul has said, a God who has given us his own Son is not going to deny us anything at all.[9] All we have to do is shake off our stupor and open our eyes afresh.

The choice is a simple one.

Back to Jesus or back to the jungle!

📖 PUBLISHED IN THE PLAIN TRUTH: OCTOBER – NOVEMBER 2006

ENDNOTES

1 Proverbs 9:10
2 John 8:44
3 Luke 5:29-30
4 Proverbs 23:29-35
5 1 Corinthians 6:18
6 Ephesians 5:1-6
7 Mark 8:36
8 Proverbs 14:34
9 Romans 8:32

Atheism is not so smart

Many years ago I discovered John Bunyan's famous book *Pilgrim's Progress*. Recently I have read it again and have been surprised to discover in it some characters I have never noticed before.

There is 'Atheist' who meets Christian and Hopeful on their way to the Celestial City. He asks where they are going and when they tell him of their hopes of heaven, 'then Atheist fell into very great laughter' explaining 'I laugh to see what ignorant people you are.' He insists, 'there is no such place as you dream of.'

There is another similar character called 'Shame', not because he feels any shame himself, but because of his habit of calling out 'Shame' whenever he meets a Christian. His view, like that of Atheist is that it is 'a pitiful, low, sneaking business for a man to mind religion.'

These two characters are not uncommon today. Secularism has become fashionable. Atheism is thought to be quite smart, whereas the media often portray believers as bigots and boobies. The same view can be found in some educational circles. I know of a school where a new head teacher has banned the Christmas crib because she says it is not 'politically correct' for a modern school to have one.

I am sure she feels smart and fashionable in having these views, and fashionable she may well be, but smart she is not.

To believe or not to believe

When I was training for the ministry, I had the good fortune to spend four years at Oxford, obtaining a degree in classics and theology, and then two years of post-graduate study in Cambridge. The purpose was to teach me to think.

If Bunyan's Atheist was right and having a Christian faith is a sign of laughable ignorance, training the clergy in this way would make no sense. It would just expose the folly of belief.

However, all I can tell you is that the effect on me was precisely the opposite. The impact of those six years was to convince me that Christian belief is well able to stand up to the most searching of thought processes.

Also I could not help noting that many others had come to the same conclusion. Think, for instance, about C S Lewis, author of the famous *Narnia* stories, who taught at both Oxford and Cambridge, and whom I was privileged to meet. He was an atheist in his earlier years but found he could not continue to be so.

Or perhaps think about Professor C E M Joad, once a frequent broadcaster on the BBC's *Brains Trust*, whose atheistic views were well known. I remember reading his book *God and Evil*, which revealed that he was slowly and painfully working his way back to believing in God, a process which was completed when he wrote his final book, *Recovery of Belief*.

The writer and broadcaster, Malcolm Muggeridge made a similar journey not long afterwards. It was meeting Mother Teresa which brought him to the point at which he realized he could no longer be an unbeliever. His book *Jesus Rediscovered* told the story of his conversion.

I have a list of some fifty former atheists who became Christians. They include politicians of both the left and the right, scientists, journalists, poets and pop singers. Also what has happened to individuals has happened to nations too.

Russia has abandoned atheistic communism and returned to the beliefs of the Orthodox Church and at this very moment something extraordinary is happening in Communist China, where every day sees perhaps 15,000 new Christians.

The logic of faith

None of this is surprising. From the dawn of human thought, men and women have felt that this remarkable universe of ours cannot be a mere accident.

If you have enjoyed *The Sound of Music*, you may remember Maria singing 'nothing comes from nothing, nothing ever could', but did you know that, when she does so, she is quoting Parmenides, who lived five centuries before Jesus?

It is hard to look at the universe and not wonder where it has come from. And what a universe it is! Think of the glory of a sunset, the loveliness of a rose, the symmetry of a snowflake. Even if creation could happen inexplicably by accident, what are we to make of all the evidence of order and design? Of beauty? Of moral laws or the visionary experience? Or of art and literature and great music? Can we contemplate any or all of these things without a sense of mystery? A sense of that which is greater than we are – greater than anything which we can conceive or understand?

In Bunyan, Atheist and Shame try to dispel these questions by mockery. However mockery is a two-edged weapon.

Laughter in heaven

C S Lewis suggested that in heaven atheism would be mentioned only as a sort of joke. Perhaps for a moment we can share the humour.

Imagine you want to buy a car. You go to a local car dealer, point to a model you fancy, and ask about its production. What if the salesman said there was no production line, no design team, and that the car happened by accident? There was an explosion in the corner of the factory and when the dust settled there it was! Wouldn't you go to another salesman?

The universe is much more complex than a car.

I am not competent to know whether those who speak about a 'big bang' are right or not, but common sense tells us that this cannot be the whole story. And what about those who prefer to talk about creation in terms of a 'steady state'?

A story was told to me of two university lecturers – one a Christian, the other an atheist. When the atheist visited the Christian he was impressed to see a working model of the solar system in the other one's house. There was a representation of the sun and around it all the planets were rotating. 'My goodness, who made that?' he asked. The Christian could not resist answering, 'I thought you believed it just happened!'

Struggle for the soul of the nation

Perhaps, however, though atheism may cause laughter in heaven, the fact that it is becoming fashionable in Britain is not such a joke.

Most of the best things in our national life come from the Christian faith. Our best laws have a Christian basis. Our education system has a Christian origin. Medical care was pioneered by Christians. That is why a number of our best hospitals and hospices are named after saints. Our traditional standards of decency and honour are based on the Christian ethic.

If we were to remove the Christian influence, the result would be sheer disaster. Yet that is what is happening.

The place of Christianity in the nation is being steadily eroded. Christian couples find it difficult to adopt or foster children. Christian teachers and medics can be disciplined and even dismissed if they show their faith. Christian hoteliers are penalized for their principles.

By contrast it has become easier, more politically correct, to be an atheist. We ask ourselves what is going wrong, but we do not wait for an answer.

During World War II there was a slogan, 'Don't you know there's a war on?' You might hear it if you broke the blackout regulations or put more than five inches of water in the bath, or tried to obtain more than your ration of food.

It is a slogan we could well revive, because there is certainly a war going on now, a war of values and belief. There is a struggle for the soul of our nation and we all have to work out where we stand.

For myself, my conviction, formed over the course of many years, is that I cannot do better than to stand with and for Jesus.

The main reason why I believe in God the Father is that I take him on trust from Jesus. Atheists have to believe they know better than Jesus.

I can't do that. Can you?

📖 PUBLISHED IN THE PLAIN TRUTH: SUMMER – AUTUMN 2014

Four fundamentals about God

My wife, Eira, tells me that it is very easy to sound technical and difficult when talking about God. In my early days in the ministry when my mind was full of the theological lectures I had to listen to during my four years at Oxford and two years at Cambridge, Eira tells me I could sometimes sound very obscure when I went into the pulpit.

So she made it her business to simplify the way in which I spoke about the basics of the Christian Faith. She still does.

She is right of course. Jesus made it his business to speak in the simplest of terms when he taught about faith and life. He knew that if nobody understood what he was saying, there really was no point in saying it.

To be simple is not the same thing as being shallow. So today, lets go back to some rock-bottom basics, things which we all ought to know about God, and all can seek to pass on to others when an opportunity arises.

God is interesting

If a sermon about God ever seems dull to us, then maybe the preacher is to blame because he or she has disregarded basic rules to communication. Or maybe we ourselves are to blame because we have not been paying proper attention.

The one thing we can be certain about is that the blame will never lie in God. All the interesting things in the world are no more than pale reflections of the God who created them.

And there is no more fascinating study in the world than the study of God. It is to that study that the Bible calls us when we are told to love God with all our mind.

Of course, often the easiest way to study God is to look at the way in which creation reflects the divine.

It's rather like the way in which we find it easier to look at the reflections of the sun in creation rather than directly at the sun's blazing light.

We enjoy looking at a rainbow with its varied colours, but none of those colours would be available to us unless the light of the sun were being reflected by them. So the world would not be interesting if it were not reflecting God's own nature.

God is up to date

When we talk of God as creator, we do not mean that at some point in the past, God pressed a button and all things came into being. We also mean that the fact we are here at all depends on God's continuing creative action.

In the past week I have been trying to work out why some people seem to feel that science has disproved religion. It certainly is not true. Science and religion ask completely different questions. Science asks, 'How do things work in this world?' By contrast theology asks, 'What's life all about and what is the meaning and the purpose of it all?'

Actually we can get by perfectly well without understanding the small print of the laws of science, but if we never ask about the meaning and purpose of our life on earth, about how we can get the best out of life and put the best into life, both we and the world will be much the poorer for it.

Others may suppose God is out of date because it is only possible to worship God in the language of the old prayer book.

It is true that if you look hard enough you will probably be able to find some prayer book services in a church not too far from your own home. Personally I thank God for it. However the majority of services use a very different idiom these days. Family services with modern hymns and guitar groups and LCD projectors are around you in abundance.

Others may think Christianity is out of date because they have met Christians whose view of life does not fit in with their own. Well, tough! Since when has it been necessary or even healthy for us all to be replicas of each other?

God is involved

It used to be common to divide life into two parts. We called them 'sacred' and 'secular'.

It was a bad division.

It implied that parts of life were of concern to God, things like going to church and saying your prayers and reading the Bible, but that other things were totally outside God's concern – things like life at work, or playing a game of darts, or just going for a walk.

Actually, if we insist on making the division, God is totally secular, interested and involved in absolutely everything, not excluding the religious bits but including absolutely everything else too. That is because you and I, everything we do, everything we are, come within the concern of the 'involved God.'

God created the whole of life, and is relevant to the whole of life. Jesus says: 'Behold I stand at the door and knock. If anyone hears my voice and opens the door, I will come in.' Of course he stands at the door of the church, but also the door of the pub, the factory, the shop, the home. As you read this article, God is standing and knocking wherever you are.

God is inexhaustible

Many years ago I met a man who told me that he really thought he had the doctrine of the Holy Trinity nicely tied up in his mind.

Sometime after this he failed his degree and had to go down from his university without any qualification at all.

In a way it served him right. He really did seem to think that he had used his own mental resources to exhaust the mysteries of God, but of course God is too big for that.

Perhaps there is a lesson for all of us in this.

We would like to cut God down to the size of something we can understand. The temptation for the theologian is to cut God down to the size of a formula. The ecclesiastic is tempted to reduce God to something the size of an institution. Some Christians are tempted to reduce God to the size of this or that religious experience. But none of it will do. God is too big, too vast, too boundless and will burst the seams of any formula, any institution, any experience we may care to dream up.

You may know the schoolboy riddle, 'How far can a rabbit run into a wood?' and the answer 'Halfway, because after that the rabbit will be running out of it.' We can apply that riddle to many things but never to God. There is no such thing as halfway to infinity.

And this is all part of Christian living and of God's total inexhaustibility. No matter how much of God we may come to know and love and adore there will always be infinitely more to know, to love and to adore.

We should continually be celebrating and enjoying this, and what personally I find so amazing is that this God of infinite might and glory, whose nature we will never totally understand, let alone exhaust, is at this moment waiting for you and me to explore a myriad of possibilities in life.

The God who is interesting finds us interesting too. The God who is up to date is concerned with your today and your tomorrow – mine too. The God who is involved wants involvement in us and from us. The God who is inexhaustible will keep seeking us as personal friends.

May God bless you as you live and grow and rejoice in everything this can mean to us day by day.

📖 PUBLISHED IN THE PLAIN TRUTH: SPRING – SUMMER 2018

PS: This was the last article Roy wrote for The Plain Truth shortly before he died in April 2018.

PART THREE:
PLAIN TRUTHS ABOUT HEALING

Does Jesus heal today?
We all know that when Jesus was on earth he healed the sick. Does he still do that today?

My first conscious experience of the healing power of Jesus happened many years ago during my days as a student at Oxford, when I prayed with a sick friend. He had lost his job because of making a stand at work on a point of Christian principle.

Soon afterwards he became ill. His doctor supposed that a mystery virus of some sort was responsible. The condition involved a loss of mobility and a lot of pain. No effective treatment could be found. His illness went on for month after month.

One day we became convinced that we should say our prayers together and that I should lay hands on him in the name of Jesus. The result was quite startling. Almost immediately his condition started to improve. Within a fortnight he was out and about, riding his bicycle around the neighbourhood. It was not long before he had found another job – a better one than the one he had lost.

Since then, during the course of 42 years in the ministry of the Church of England, I have seen scores of people find healing through the power of Jesus and have written books which tell their stories.

Those who know me will tell you that I am a very ordinary Christian. I am not a person of heroic faith and do not possess any mysterious psychic gifts of healing. So healing can sometimes take me by surprise.

But viewed logically, the Ministry of Christian Healing should not surprise us.

Jesus healed the sick

When Jesus walked about the dusty roads of Palestine at the beginning of the first millennium, one of the best known and regularly reported facts about him was that he healed the sick.

If you open your own Bible casually, anywhere in one of the four Gospels, the odds are that you will find yourself reading a story about his ministry of healing. Many people were healed in his presence. A great number were healed physically – blind people, deaf people, lame people, people with terrible skin diseases, and more besides.

Some were healed mentally. There was, for instance, a spectacular occasion on which Jesus met a deranged man in a graveyard and restored him totally to his right mind.

People were also healed emotionally and spiritually, so that their attitudes and relationships and lifestyles were never the same again. There were cheats and murderers amongst his followers. Today we know them as 'saints' but they were anything but saintly before they encountered the healing power of Jesus.

Not a non-event

Jesus was never a non-event. He always made a difference to people who were open to his influence. It was as if, just as some people are infectious with disease, so Jesus was infectious with wholeness for those around him – wholeness of body, mind and spirit.

You can't resist the thought that we could certainly do with him around today. But it is as precisely as we say that to ourselves, that the Ministry of Christian Healing becomes relevant. For it is the claim of the Christian Faith that Jesus is not dead and gone and lost for ever. Christianity teaches that Jesus is available to us here and now.

We know he lived 2,000 years ago. There is no doubt that Jesus is a solid historical figure, referred to by both Christian and non-Christian writers in the ancient world.

We know that he was put to death because in a sleazy world the sort of goodness which Jesus radiated is uncomfortable to live with, and so the authorities whipped up a lynch-mob to howl for his blood and he was executed on a cross.

But just as there is overwhelming historical evidence for his life and death, so there is massive evidence that after he had been put to death by a Roman execution squad, subsequently the world was amazed to find that he was vibrantly alive again.

Hundreds saw him. Thousands of lives were immediately changed by him. Millions have continued to be changed by him over the centuries that followed. For Jesus was not just a good man. He was much more. Mysteriously, he was God's way of coming to the rescue of a planet and a people gone wrong. And he and his living influence are available today – he promised as much himself. Listen to the plain truth as Jesus told it:

Abundant life

He promised to transform the lives of all who took him seriously. 'I came,' he said, 'that they may have life and have it abundantly'. And he gave this pledge to his followers for all time: 'Where two or three are gathered together in my name, I am there among them.' So when Christians come together it is not just to meet each other, but also to meet him. And the Bible tells us that when we meet him today we shall find he has not changed. 'He is the same yesterday, today and for ever.' So if he healed those who were sick in body, mind and spirit 2,000 years ago, and if we can meet him now, it must logically follow that Jesus can heal today.

It is one of the most exciting facts about Christianity in the world today, as we prepare to move into a third millennium, that all the Christian churches are now beginning to rediscover the healing power of Jesus Christ.

Those who welcome this rediscovery include many doctors. One wrote to me only a few days ago telling me of her enthusiastic support for the Christian Healing Ministry.

Quacks and charlatans?

Mind you, it should also be said that spiritual healing can go wrong. It is possible for a healing ministry to be faked by quacks and charlatans. And even those who are totally sincere can make mistakes. Also in something as mysterious as spiritual healing there are bound to be problems to be faced and questions to be raised. I will try to deal with some of them in the next issue of this magazine.[1]

But for now, may I suggest a simple prayer exercise which you may like to undertake either alone or with one or two friends. Even if you feel that your personal level of Christian commitment is hesitant and low-grade, don't be discouraged.

If there is any real sense at all in which you put your trust in Jesus, try this out. It cannot do you any harm – and it may make a major difference to you and to those you love.

First, remember the promise which Jesus made to his disciples at the end of his life on Earth. 'I am with you always, even to the end of the world.' Claim this promise for yourself and picture Jesus looking at you as you look at him. His gaze is full of love, not sentimental indulgent love, but realistic, costly, healing, saving love. That love is vibrant with the re-creative power of God. Picture and feel his hands upon you. Know that his will is for your wholeness.

Be prepared for him to teach you about yourself. He may show you some element in your life, some practice or thought pattern which should not be there. If so, put it in his hands. Allow him to take it away. Do not protect it against him.

Pray the words 'Your holy and healing will be done' and ask for the strength to mean these words more and more. Know that Jesus is not only *at* your side. He is also *on* your side. He wants only the best for you in body, mind and spirit.

Then when you have spent some time in his presence, bring all whom you care about into that presence too. You do not have to do anything. Just stand by as Jesus looks at your friend, your neighbour, your loved one. Quietly and confidently align your will with his, as you picture him speaking and touching the one for whom you are praying.

Why not do this every day till the next issue of this magazine? You may be surprised at the effect it will have upon you and on others through you. Christian prayer is never a non-event, because Christ himself is never a non-event.

Only this morning before I wrote these words, I received a letter from a couple with whom I prayed a few months ago.

The wife has a manic-depressive problem and the marriage has been under stress. But this morning's letter says, 'We are so grateful for your prayers. The process of healing is very evident now.'

May God grant you similar evidence of the healing power of Jesus in the weeks ahead.

📖 PUBLISHED IN THE PLAIN TRUTH: APRIL – MAY 1999.

ENDNOTES

1 You can read the follow-on article to this – *When healing does not come* – *on the next page.*

• Scripture references throughout this article: John 10:10; Matthew 18:10; Hebrews 13:8; Matthew 28:20.

When healing does *not* come...

In my last article (*Does Jesus heal today?*), I invited you to rediscover the healing power of Jesus and suggested a prayer method to help you do so. It would be good to hear from any of you who tried it. My guess is that many of you will have found it a good and positive healing experience. If so, I'm truly glad for you. Hold on to the truths you have discovered. Keep practising the presence of Christ.

But some may be feeling puzzled or let down, because, as I wrote last time, 'In something as mysterious as spiritual healing, there are bound to be problems to be faced and questions to be raised.'

So let's face one of them today.

What about people who sincerely bring some trouble to the Lord in prayer and ask that it should be removed – only to find that afterwards it seems as bad as ever? During my many years as a vicar, people have come to our church asking for the ministry of Christian Healing for all sorts of reasons. Some have come with severe illnesses like cancer or multiple sclerosis, others with crippling depression or some other form of mental pain; others with a relationship problem, perhaps a marriage in danger of breaking down.

But not always

Sometimes amazing things have happened. I have seen some supposedly incurable cancers disappear and multiple sclerosis go into what seems to be permanent remission. I have seen depression lift and marriage problems solved. But there have also been many other occasions when cancer, multiple sclerosis, depression and marriage problems have remained unhealed.

So the question has to be asked: If the ministry of Christian Healing sometimes brings us all we ask for, why does it not always do so? What can I say to you if you have prayed for healing and healing has not come?

Let me tell you four things I would *not* say.

First, I would *not* accuse you of not having enough faith. That would be a cruel thing to do. It would also be unscriptural. When I offer the ministry of Healing to someone in need, the onus of faith is on me, as the ministrant, not on the person to whom I am ministering.

Jesus says, 'Those who believe shall lay hands on the sick' not 'Hands shall be laid on those who believe.' When Jesus laid hands on Jairus' daughter, she was in a deep and death-like coma. She could not have exercised faith at the time. But the touch and the word and the faith of Jesus brought her back to life. It brings to mind a moment in my own ministry when I was asked if I could possibly do anything for a woman, a senior and long-standing member of our church, who was at that time in a deep and seemingly terminal coma in one of our local hospitals.

Whilst her husband wept in a little room next to the ward, I was allowed to go in and see her apparently lifeless body. I asked the ward sister if it would do any harm if I were to try to offer the ministry of Christian Healing.

I remember her answer: 'It won't do any harm, but it can't do any good.' She continued, 'This one is as good as dead.' I prayed and laid hands on her in the name of Jesus, and amazingly the supposed corpse sat up. She went on to live for another six years and had a good quality of life. In fact, from then on she seemed healthier than she had been for quite a while.

I am telling you the story here, not because it is a rather sensational one, but because it makes the point that, though she was a woman of faith, she was certainly not in a position to exercise her faith at the moment of healing.

Secondly, I would *not* jump to the conclusion that, if there are no tangible results, then any minister you may have approached must be a quack or a charlatan. Quacks and charlatans do exist – but not many. Most who offer the Christian Healing Ministry are men and women of God, sincere in what they do, and anguished when it seems to fail.

Mind you, having said that, it is right to be selective about those from whom you seek help. Not all spiritual healing is *Christian* Healing, relying on the presence of Christ. Some healers rely on very different resources and not all of them are desirable. So it is always wise to ask, 'What comes with this package?' If the answer is anything but the power of Jesus, we may want to have second thoughts about exposing ourselves to the forces involved.

Also, even if the name of Jesus is well to the front, one or two things should perhaps sometimes start warning bells ringing in our minds. Be wary of any who seem to give the impression that their healing ministry never fails. I know of no one in the Christian Healing Ministry who has not experienced failure from time to time – and that even includes Jesus! We are told that his power to work miracles was restricted in Nazareth because of the negative attitude towards him there. You should also be wary of any who in cases of failure seek to place the blame on their clients.

This brings me to the third thing which I would *not* say. I would never say, 'If you are not healed, it must be because you do not deserve to be healed.'

Christian blessings never rest upon what we deserve. They are God's gifts and stem from his love. Think, for instance, about forgiveness. Jesus has come to offer forgiveness and a way back to God not because of our merits, but because of our needs. 'While we were yet sinners Christ died for us.' Christian Healing is like that. It is a response to need, not a seal of approval.

Fourthly I would *not* say, 'Whether or not you deserve to be healed, it is clear that God has decided not to heal on this occasion. So you must just be humble enough to accept your illness as his will.'

It is never that simple.

God has revealed himself as 'the Lord who heals' and he is totally self-consistent. In him there is 'no variability, no shadow cast by turning'. If he is sometimes the Lord who heals, he is always the Lord who heals. However, if human history shows us anything, it teaches that God's will is not always done in the short run.

Mystery of suffering

There is a mystery about suffering, just as there is a mystery about healing.

This is one of the themes of the Book of Job. Job is a pious family man and is wealthy and healthy until Satan strikes him down. Poor Job loses his health, his wealth and his family. His friends come round and advise him to try to understand, because if he can fathom why these things have happened, he will be able to amend his life and all will be well.

Job knows that his situation is nothing as simple as that. He and his friends argue themselves to a standstill, and it is at that point that God finally speaks.

Strangely, he says nothing about Job's sufferings but takes him on a tour of creation and helps him to see the mystery of it all.

Finally Job makes the discovery for himself that, if there are mysteries in creation, there must be other mysteries too – including the mystery of suffering. He stops trying to understand. He settles for a sense of mystery.

At the end of the story, he finds new wealth, new health and a new family. But he finds he has to learn from his direct encounter with God. *There are times when our trust has to be greater than our understanding.*

So suppose you find a church near you which takes the ministry of Christian Healing seriously (as more and more churches do these days), and suppose you go along to a healing service or to some other activity at which there is healing prayer, or suppose you ask for healing ministry at a personal one-to-one level. What can you realistically expect?

Tangible benefit

My belief is that those who are open to receive Christian Healing should *always* expect to receive strengthening and blessing from this ministry.

But there may be a more tangible benefit than that. Afterwards we may be somehow different, more whole in some way. And whether our experience of healing is total or partial, whether it affects our body, mind or spirit, we will have no doubt about its reality and its importance. Just occasionally it can be so extraordinary that the word 'miracle' may come to mind.

However the greatest benefit does not lie in any of these things. It lies quite simply in drawing nearer to Jesus. There is nothing more precious than the experience of his presence. His company, his care, and his influence are infinitely desirable for their own sake – for his own sake.

Of course there will be by-products if we draw nearer to him, because the Son of God never was and never can be a non-event. But if we are wise, we will not focus on the by-products that result from his presence. In fact if healing comes to us, we may not even notice the moment of its coming. For the eyes of our spirit will be on him and not on ourselves, which, as the Bible tells us, is the secret of life at its fullest and best – just 'looking to Jesus, the pioneer and perfecter of our faith'.

📖 PUBLISHED IN THE PLAIN TRUTH: JUNE – JULY 1999.

• Scripture references throughout this article: Mark 16:18, Matthew 15:23-28, Romans 5:8, Exodus 15:26, James 1:17, Hebrews 12:2, Luke 8:49-56

Inner healing

F ew things are more precious in life than a sense of inner peace. Even if we are going through times of darkness and difficulty, as long as we have a still centre at the core of our being, this will help us to 'keep calm and carry on.'

The problem is that inner peace can sometimes be a fragile thing. There are perhaps three big threats that can destroy it. They are GUILT, ANGER and FEAR.

The good news is that the Christian Faith can help us deal with all these threats and show us how to discover inner healing, if we rest in its truth.

Guilt

Actually I hope that there are certain things that do make us feel guilty. The Bible tells us again and again that we are all sinners: 'All have sinned and fall short of the glory of God' (Romans 3:23), 'If we say we have no sin, we deceive ourselves and the truth is not in us' (1 John 1:8).

To the men who were about to stone a woman taken in adultery, Jesus said, 'Let him who has no sin throw the first stone' (John 8:7), and at these words they had the grace to slink away.

If you find that a sense of guilt is disturbing your inner peace, you may be surprised to know that my first word to you is 'congratulations'. Don't feel guilty about feeling guilty. We could do with more guilt in society – not less.

So what is the Christian answer to the loss of peace that can be caused by a sense of guilt?

Society thinks that the answer to the distress that guilt can cause is to be found in the concept of *permissiveness*, but society is wrong. Permissiveness tells us that sin is not really all that sinful and that a little of what you fancy does you good, irrespective of whether it is right or wrong. Permissiveness hides behind a winking, smirking mask. However, if we look behind the mask, there is not really much to smirk about. There is little perceptiveness, little healing, little awareness of the laws of cause and effect here.

By contrast the Christian Faith points us not to the concept of permissiveness but to that of *forgiveness*, which is totally different.

Forgiveness sees things exactly as they are and knows all about the laws of cause and effect. It does not pretend that there is no difference between right and wrong. It knows that we cannot break God's laws with impunity.

However, it also knows that God's capacity for love is greater than our capacity for sin and folly, and that amazingly God is prepared to pay the price for staying in relationship with us through all that Jesus has done for us on the cross.

It is when we open ourselves to that forgiveness that God's love is able to bring healing to the deepest places of our being.

We do not fancy owning up to those flaws and follies which disturb our peace, but it is when we make our way to the foot of the cross and ask for forgiveness that we begin to rediscover inner wholeness and sometimes to experience a new physical wholeness too.

I well remember Joanna, whose skin rash cleared up before my eyes, when she found forgiveness for a sin long since past.

So I wonder whether this might be the moment for an act of repentance and confession at the foot of the cross for someone reading these words.

It may not be an enjoyable prayer. It may involve some pain for the moment. But it could be the means of discovering a new inner healing which will make any temporary discomfort more than worthwhile.

Anger

This is a world with a great deal of anger in it. There is probably much more anger in you and me than we may realize.

If I am leading a conference and am having difficulty in starting a group discussion, I have learned that a sure-fire way of doing so is to ask the group members what are the sort of things that irritate them most. There is rarely a shortage of response to that.

One reason why we do not always recognize the amount of anger around us and in us is that it shows itself in many different ways. Sometimes it shows itself in its true colours – a fit of temper, complete with clenched fists, clenched teeth, red face, raised voice and raised blood pressure. But sometimes it is partly held in check and so little more than low-grade resentment shows on the surface.

Sometimes it is completely repressed. It becomes the unconscious background to a feeling of black depression. It can turn itself into a physical symptom – a headache, a stomach ulcer, tightness across the chest, a fast and bumpy heart.

It can be completely misdirected – taken out on quite the wrong person. It can be dangerous in all sorts of ways, even leading to an attempt at suicide if we allow it to do a U-turn and to focus back on ourselves.

I well remember Greg, whom I managed to pull back from the verge of suicide by helping him to become aware of his anger and of the fact that there was a remedy for it at the heart of the Christian Gospel.

What then is this remedy?

It is a strange one and may surprise you. Archbishop Robert Leighton[1] once put it into an unforgettable phrase: 'We Christians are privileged,' he said, 'to vent our rage into the bosom of God.' It would seem that much anger, if we would only admit it, is at root a desire to rage at God. He created us. He put us into a world where there are many troubles, and though he did not create those troubles, nonetheless for reasons which we often cannot understand he allows them.

However, Christianity is unique among world religions in teaching that God allows us to be totally honest with him about how this makes us feel. We can do exactly as Archbishop Leighton says. If we feel uneasy about this, we can at any rate know that it is a thoroughly Biblical process. Listen to Moses raging against God in the eleventh chapter of the Book of Numbers:

> *'Lord why have you treated me so badly? Why have you given me responsibility for all these people? I can't be responsible…it's too much. …if you are going to treat me like this, KILL ME so that I won't have to endure your cruelty any longer!!'*

There are many instances of anger against God in the Bible. Elijah, Job, Jonah, Jeremiah and others too all rage against God. The Book of Lamentations could be renamed 'The Book of Raging' – have a look at the opening verses of chapter three, for instance.

So if you have identified anger in yourself, be honest to God about it. Let it rip when you say your prayers. If you are doing it under the surface, you might as well come clean about it.

Even if you find yourself hammering the nails into the hands of the Son of God and ramming on the crown of thorns, re-crucifying Christ, amazingly he will still love you, and your rage and all its destructive power will drain away, as you realize, in the words of Joy Riordan, that 'God is a very safe person to be angry with.'

Fear

Psychotherapist Harry Guntrip used to teach that the greatest enemy of life at its fullest and best is fear.

Like anger, fear can show itself in many ways. Sometimes it directs itself at something specific like a forthcoming operation. Sometimes the cause makes no sense at all, like a fear of open spaces or of something as harmless as moths. Sometimes there seems no object at all, but the fearfulness is just present deep inside us.

Different people come into my mind. Milly is a natural worrier. If there is nothing to worry about, she will invent something. Dave becomes aggressive because of his fearfulness. On the other hand Poppy cannot bear to be ignored. She has to be the centre of attention. At first she looks confident, but after a while you start to see the anxiety under the surface. Or there is Alexander who is afraid of relationships, afraid of being hurt, and so always keeps his distance. The good news is that just as the Christian Faith can deal with guilt and anger so it provides the resources to deal with fearfulness.

God can heal our fear by a miracle of identification through Jesus.

When life is at its lowest and darkest point, we can discover Jesus in the depths. He is a saviour who comes to us *from below*. Even in times of total dereliction and despair, we can encounter the one who himself experienced dereliction on the cross and who has promised, 'I am with you always'.[2]

His presence has always been a healing presence.

It is still so.

We love the 23rd Psalm because we rightly apply its words to Jesus, our own good shepherd. It is so good to be able to say to him: 'Yea, though I walk through the valley of the shadow of death, I will fear no evil, for thou art with me,' and to know that this applies not just to the moment of physical death but to the most deadly experiences that this life can afford.

In the words of the Good News Bible, 'Even though I go through the deepest darkness, I will not be afraid, Lord. For you are with me.'

It is a truth to test for ourselves.

...and so to prayer

The odds are that you and I all need some measure of interior healing, but millions have found that Jesus can bring it to us.

His promise rings through the ages: 'In me you may have peace.'[3] We discover it both as we stand at his side and as we kneel at his cross. Here is a prayer which embodies that discovery:

> *Lord, I thank you that you know me better than I know myself, and I thank you that though I am far from lovable, you still love me with all your heart. Thank you for this love and for the healing it can bring me. Help me to accept it into the very core of my being. Let your holy and healing will be done in each one of us – beginning in this life and then blossoming into eternity. Alleluia. Amen.*

📖 PUBLISHED IN THE PLAIN TRUTH: SPRING 2014

ENDNOTES

1   Robert Leighton (1611 – 25 June 1684) was a Scottish prelate and scholar, best known as a church minister, Bishop of Dunblane, Archbishop of Glasgow, and Principal of the University of Edinburgh from 1653 to 1662. He was noted for his Christian piety, his humility and gentleness, and his devotion to his calling.
2   Matthew 28:20
3   John 16:33

A PRAYER FOR THE PLAIN TRUTH
By Revd Roy Lawrence

Father, we pray for all who
speak where many listen
and write what many read.

Especially we pray for
The Plain Truth.
May it be both plain and true.

Let its lay-out please our eyes
and its contents feed our souls.

Here let the voice of
Jesus be heard.
Here let the light of
Jesus be seen.

As we read its message,
bless us, Lord,
And through us let
the world be blessed.

In the name of Christ,

Amen.